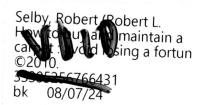

How to Buy and Maintain a Carpet

Avoid Losing a Fortune When Buying a Carpet!

by Robert L. Selby

Ross Books
P.O. Box 4340
Berkeley, Ca 94704
www.rossbooks.com

DEDICATION

As I undertook the task of writing this book, and it was a task, it was my desire to present those important facts that would aid and inform but most of all save the consumer money. These facts are presented in a simple, easily understood, and occasionally humorous manner. It is not my intention to impress others with what I know, but rather, taking what I know and making it easy for them too know.

As this is the first book of its kind (to my knowledge), ever written to the consumer, there was very little material to draw on. Books and pamphlets that are directed toward the industry are of little use to the general public. Searching libraries and bookstores for additional input only benefited this work slightly. The experts in the various fields were truly informed in those fields;

However, I could find none that had any real experience in an adjoining field. For instance, the carpet manufacturers had not seen the carpet they made that was ten years old-having been cleaned 8 or 9 times...And been lived on by two different families, both with children and pets. Consequently, because of their limited knowledge, I could not use much of their advice. The trouble with most expertise, is that it has been born under laboratory conditions and, therefore, only completely valid in that laboratory.

So, most of what is covered has been a result of nearly 10 years of my own experiences and research, all of which I dedicate to you, the consumer. My only apology is for not having the literary talent of william shakespeare. But I do take consolation in knowing that had he possessed this book while out buying or cleaning his carpet, he could have certainly saved a sixpence or two.

PREFACE

In the late 1940's, the wall to wall carpet industry was small and for the most part far from the reach of the general population. The floors that were covered were hotel and theater lobbies, only the plushest of executive suites and a few luxurious homes of the wealthy. The prices were high, much too expensive for most of us. Even if we could afford it, the availability was limited, for the carpet stores were only in large cities and very few at that. Those that did manage to install carpeting had yet another problem, cleaning. The professional carpet cleaners were even harder to find than the retailer.

Though our floors were wood or linoleum or asphalt tile, our desire was to some day have them covered with carpet. Americans have always found a way of gaining their desires. So along with new techniques in carpet manufacturing, synthetic fiber developments and a tremendous consumer demand, the industry exploded in the 50's. Starting with a handful of mills in the early days to hundreds today. Retail carpet stores, numbering 34,000 are in every town and hamlet with over 19,000 carpet cleaners out cleaning the billions of square feet of carpeting that is on this nation's floors.

Even the little corner market rents the (do-it-yourself) carpet cleaning machines, while large supermarket chains merchandise literally thousands of different carpet care products annually. Every newspaper will run ads several times a week for carpet sales or cleaning specials.

Today, nearly everyone has carpeting in their homes. Ifs still expensive, in fact it will be the third largest investment the average homeowner makes during their lifetime. The actual cost is not just the purchase price which is expensive but the major expense is the maintenance, which is many times greater than the original purchase cost. Vacuum cleaners and bags, repairs, spills, stains, floods, professional cleaning, hours and hours of vacuuming then finally replacement, starting the cycle all over again.

Carpet is a good investment. Its qualities and benefits far outweigh anything bad that may be said about it. However, with the great boom in the industry also came the thousands of people to run that industry.

The more people, the more incompetence and worse yet, the more dishonesty.

Sure i could yell for the government to step in to certify and regulate this industry. But don't we have too much government already? If they did come in, their regulations would force up the cost of carpet while forcing the small businessman out of business especially the honest ones. Instead, let's educate ourselves. There is not that much to learn, but what can be learned will be our protection. Your knowledge of the products you buy is the only real protection you have anyway. It is the knowledgeable and learned that prevent the dishonest and greedy from landing at our doorstep. This then is the reason for my book. It will arm you with all that is needed to protect yourself. Read and enjoy.

Contents

PART I
General Information   9

PART II
Purchase   31

PART III
Maintenance   95

VACUUMING

PART I
General Information

BRIEF HISTORY OF CARPETING

Rugs and floor covering material must date back as far as man himself. It's not hard to imagine early man, after jumping out of a warm bed in the morning, wanting to land his feet on something other than dirt or stone floor. Or at dinner time, before the table was in wide use, he certainly would have wanted to sit on at least a towel or something. Besides, where would he be able to sweep the dirt? So it is reasonable to assume that man has used some form of floor covering in his home for quite a while now.

Man as he is, has an inherent ability to improve his surroundings. Especially if he can make a couple of bucks on the side while doing it. So as he started out making some rugs for the family, some new technology entered in, making it possible now to weave with cloth, (cotton, wool, flax, jute, silk and animal hair). So in just a few hundred years the product of rugs had gone from the reed mats to the cloth mats. Well, something happened at that time, probably wine spilled on a white rug or somebody squashed a berry into the plain colored fabric. In any case the colored carpet was born. After a few hundred more years, rug making and cloth dying was a real art, everyone on the block had their own weavers loom, and business was hopping. Rugs were used every where, home, office, tent and even in the tombs of the dead.

By the 5th Century A.D. rug making began taking on the designs and characteristics, that we know as the Oriental Rug. As different tribes learned to tie these rugs together, it wasn't to long before they were putting their names on them—not their personal names but their tribal names which represented their tribal standard. This standard was sometimes a flag or ornament that was placed outside the chiefs door.

As time went by, the standards may have remained the same but the design on the rugs were getting prettier with each adaptation to the improved standard. Eventually these rugs were identified by the location or town in which they were made— with mainly 6 different groups of the Oriental rugs: Persian (Iran), Turkish, Turkman (Russian), Caucasian (Russian), Chinese, and Indian (India). India and China did not seem to follow the lead in designing their carpets after their forefathers but rather after time periods of rulership in their countries. There were also Moslem prayer rugs that were distinctively different from the others in that each rug has a direction pattern woven into it—the bearer of the rug, when he prays towards Mecca, has a place for his feet on one end and the other end is faced to the east.

But on to the progress of carpeting! The MOORS, who were forcing their way upon the Western civilizations with bloodshed, pillage and plunder, also brought with them the art of rugmaking. As all "hot, new ideas" go, somebody always gets the wrong idea and uses their new found knowledge to do something else with it.

So the FRENCH came up with the TAPESTRY. I guess they'd rather walk

on cold floors and have warm walls. In any case, that didn't last too long. They finally got with the program and started doing some of their own rug work. And wouldn't you know it, the French were the first to organize a carpet-makers club called "The Carpet makers Guild" which was formed in Paris around 1450.

Later on the French gained prominence with two rug products: The AUBUSSON & SAVONNERIE. Aubusson was named after the town in which they were made. Savonnerie was named after a soap factory which was converted to a rug factory.

The British and French have always competed, and rug making provided for yet one more field for the two to out-do one another.

King Edward III of England heard rumors that the French were decorating their floors with home made, rather than imported rugs. So by a little coersion, bribery and skulldugery, he convinced a couple of French rugmakers to cross the Channel and spill the beans of the trade. Once this information became known the English wasted no time in setting up their own rug factories and competing on the international market. But the real carpet breakthrough came when the British copied a technique used in Brussels for tapestries, and converted it over to carpet. Thus was the Wilton Weave.

The Americans weren't standing idle. In 1791 in Philadelphia, they established the first factory for weaving yarn carpeting. Then in 1804 another was built in Worcester, Massachusetts. Then somebody in Lowell, Massachusetts, decided they were tired of making rugs by hand. They invented a way in which a steam engine might be attached to the loom—behold the POWER LOOM (around 1839).

Then another American, ERASTUS BIGELOW made some important improvements on it and rugs started getting mass produced. In 1836 HALCYON SKINNER, another American, perfected a power-driven AXMINSTER LOOM.

By this time there were four major weaves being used in the industry. Three of which are still in use today, in woven wool carpets...These are...

VELVET WEAVE: The simplest weave used mostly for solid-colored carpet. Nearly all the basic carpet styles available today are made possible with the velvet weave.

The STUFFER and SHOT are the two cross (intercrossed with one another) strings by which the pile fabric is woven. The CHAIN is that independent string that secures the weave and holds the pile into place.

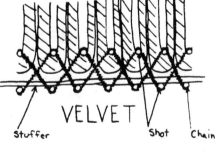

WILTON WEAVE: Woven on a specialized loom that raises yarns of the desired color to form a pattern, and at the same time leave the other yarns buried in the pile of the carpet. Loom wires make loops in the warp yarns, thus producing the pile of the carpet. With the Wilton weave loom, they can make intricate designs and

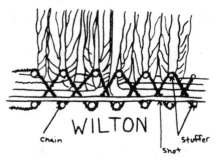

different texture variations in the pile of the carpet. However, the use of many colors is not available with the Wilton.

AXMINSTER WEAVE: Patterns and colors are unlimited. The actual weaving process is similar to the handmade Orientals in that each tuft of pile yarn is inserted into the warp weave separately. One distinctive characteristic of the Axminster is that because of its unusual weaving it may be rolled up lengthwise but not crosswise.

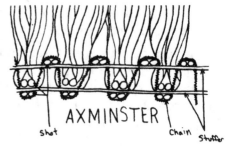

After the development of the power loom the industry stayed basically the same until the mid 1940's when the tufting machine was adapted to carpet manufacturing. This is discussed in more detail on page 10.

Carpets today are made with both natural and man-made fibers.

THE NATURAL FIBERS

COTTON: Cotton is not widely used in the carpet industry today except in throw rugs and in some rare instances, for the secondary backing. However, it is so important as a fiber, it is included in this manual.

Cotton is vegetable in nature, and the fibers are a protective device for the seeds of the plant. The plant itself grows in many of the warmer areas of the world. After the fibers are picked, they are separated and spun together, then treated with caustic soda and tension is applied. The fiber swells up and becomes permanently straight.

Cotton fibers are strong—more so when. wet than dry. They are very absorbent. Other qualities are: heat resistant, cleans well, and durable.

It is believed that cotton first was used in India but the Chinese developed the first spinning wheel. From there the use of cotton spread throughout the world. During the Industrial Revolution, weaving techniques were improved but it wasn't until the industry took off in the USA during the 1700's with "Eli Whitney's" invention of his cotton gin, the machine that revolutionized the cotton industry. The gin separated the fiber from the seeds. This was done by hand before that. Cotton production jumped over 400% in 20 years. Today the USA still is a major producer of cotton and cotton fabrics.

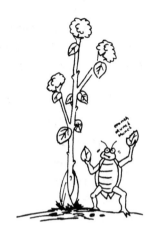

WOOL: The protective coat on sheep. It is similar to human hair except when examined under a microscope, the fiber has the appearance of fish scales. These scales aid in the fiber adhesiveness when spun.

Wool has differing qualities and one way to get the best quality wool is to compare the number of scales. There may be as many as 3000 or as few as 500 scales per fiber. The one with the most is considered the best.

The fiber is strong, elastic, resilient. It has a natural waviness to it making it appear bulky. It's a great insulator, has a high absorption rate, but is affected by moth and mildew.

How do we get fibers? Steal it from the sheep. In fact, every year or every other year, the wool is sheared, bagged and sorted. The best wool comes from the back and side of the head. All wool is sorted into as many as 40 different grades from just one fleece.

The wool then is cleaned, separated into like grades of wool, spun, twisted and stretched into yarn. The kinks are removed with heat and depending on the circumstance, the fiber is dyed somewhere in between these steps. Now the carpet is ready to be woven.

WOOLENS—WORSTEDS: What is the difference between woolens and worsteds? Worsteds are handled similarly to woolens except a few other processes are added such as combing and the fiber lengths are made uniform. These two processes allow wool to be made stronger by twisting. They also give it a smoother and more uniform appearance.

The wools chosen for worsteds are, on the whole, a better grade of wool. They are lighter in weight than a woolen and the wearability is better. They should last longer.

Once the yarn is made and the material woven, it is shrunk before it is made into garments. In yarn used for carpeting, it is shrunk before the carpet is woven.

Wool carpets are considered even today by many as the finest around. In fact many of these carpets (that were usually installed back in the 20's and 30's) are still being used. The problem today is that wool has gotten so expensive that the average home owner just can't afford them, thereby forcing most of us to the less expensive synthetic carpets.

JUTE: Comes from the Jute plant. This plant averages 10 to 15 feet in height with fibers as long as 7 feet. Chemically it is cellulose. It is strong and yellow-brown in color, dissolves in water, and has poor elasticity. Because of the poor elasticity it is used to bind things together. Therefore, for years has been a great fiber for holding together and giving strength to carpets.

Today, jute is rapidly being replaced by man-made fibers that are equally as strong but are lighter, cheaper, not susceptible to moisture, and are not affected by weather.

The major producers of jute in the world are fastly coming under communist control, thus making it harder to get and more expensive.

THE MAN-MADE FIBERS

The process of manufacturing these fibers is a simulation of the silkworm making its thin strands of silk.

The silkworm forces through its glandular structure a liquid which, as it makes contact with the air, becomes a solid elongated filament. Scientists have observed this being done and developed a mechanical method to reproduce this action. They also invented a substance to replace the liquid that the silkworm emitted. Rather than forcing this new substance through glands, they made a mechanical device called a SPINNERET which looks and acts similar to a shower head—as the fibers are formed and extruded from the spinneret, they are stretched (a process called drawing) to add strength and elasticity to the fibers.

RAYON: The most perfected and ready to manufacture artificial silk. There are so many men who are responsible for Rayon, it would do no good to mention any. It made its appearance in 1889 at the Paris Exhibition.

Rayon was the first major man-made fiber. It is a textile fiber made from chemically treated cellulose from natural sources (either wood pulp or cotton linters). Presently "pine wood" is the major raw material in Rayon.

Rayon gets its name from an industry-sponsored contest in 1924. Up until this time it had been known as artificial silk.

The Rayon fibers are strong and very absorbant (like cotton). These qualities make it very susceptible to dyes. It is slow to dry. Although Rayon is man-made, it does not melt when burned. It will burn at high temperatures, however. It is moth-proof and not affected by the average household chemicals (such as bleach).

Rayon has experienced ups and downs in its popularity because of competition with other fibers. It is used today in nearly all areas of the textile industry including carpeting: both with the carpet backing and in the pile surface by interweaving it with other fibers.

ACETATE: First came out in the mid-1860's but was not really perfected until 1920 by British Celanese Limited.

In the past RAYON & ACETATE FIBERS were grouped together as one because they both use "regenerated cellulose" from trees and/or cotton. However, today the acetate fiber is separate because its final properties are distinctively different from that of Rayon.

It gets its name from "acetic acid." The major components are wood pulp or the cotton linters (cellulose) which are treated with chemicals with the results being an entirely different substance called "cellulose acetate." It dose not resemble cotton or wood cellulose.

The cellulose acetate is sent through the spinneret and processed much like the other man-made fibers. Its fiber shape can be made in any way desirable. By varying the shapes, different coloring effects or dirt-hiding characteristics are achieved. The over-all appearance of a finished product will be determined by the shape of the fibers coming out of the Spinneret, either round, oblong, square, flat, thick, thin, smooth. It can even be made to curl or kink up.

Acetate is not very absorbant. The fast drying fibers are soft and resilient. It resists wrinkling and has a "spring-back-into-shape" property, it is resistant to moth, mildew, and mold. It may be dyed but not as easily as Rayon.

Acetate fibers are used in nearly all the general textile areas including carpeting.

NOTE OF IMPORTANCE: If acetate fiber is used in your carpet, do not use alcohol or acetone chemicals (nail polish remover or perfume) as these will dissolve the fibers.

NYLON: (Polyamide Fibers) - Invented by Dr. W. H. Carothers. It began as "FIBER 66" until du Pont Company patented the process and soon it was to become a household word.

The fibers are synthetically made from some basic chemicals that are found in things like coal, oil, oats, bran, even corncobs.

The manufacture of nylon fibers is very sophisticated and technical. Therefore, I have reduced it into a very simple form.

Step 1: Two different chemicals are mixed together to form a product called "NYLON SALT."

Step 2: The salt is then dissolved with water.

Step 3: Then the water is evaporated.

Step 4: The salt is placed in a big pressure cooker (called an AUTO-CLAVE) and heated up. The heating causes the molecular structure to change to the point that it now has a structural characteristic similar to wood and silk.

Step 5: It is then taken out of the Autoclave, cooled off, hardened, and chopped up into small particles.

Step 6: These particles are placed in the spinneret and melted and drawn the same as the other man-made fibers.

Nylon is stronger, yet lighter in weight, than any other commonly used fiber. It is elastic and resilient; is nonabsorbent and therefore, quick drying. It is, in itself, dirt resistant because dirt does not hold onto it. It is moth and insect proof; water, mold, mildew, and most cleaning chemicals do not affect it. Overall it is a highly durable fiber.

Its uses are probably the most of all fibers including the bulk of the carpet industry.

TWO NOTABLE NYLON FIBERS —"Antron III (tm)" This new concept in fiber design with built-in static control will hide dirt more effectively than any previous fiber. "Anso IV (tm)" Also new, has incorporated a soil retardant into the actual manufacturing of the fiber. This is not to be confused with soil retardant coatings applied after the fiber has been made. Though this is a very new innovation and has not been out long enough to see if it will work for years under actual use, all indications point to this fiber as being a major break-through for carpet maintenance.

POLYESTER: The first fibers in England were under the trade name of TERYLENE by The Calico Printers Association. Then in 1946 du Pont Company secured the exclusive right to produce it in the U.S.

The production of Polyester is quite similar to that of Nylon except the chemical components are all together different. The various chemicals needed are put into a vacuum container and cooked at high temperature until they are formed into a hard substance (porcelain like). Then the spinneret process is used.

Polyester is extremely resilient either wet or dry. It is nonabsorbent and impervious to moisture. It is lightweight, resistant to sunlight and weather. It is strong and mothproof. It is used in nearly all textile products, including carpeting. It is interwoven with other man-made fibers to strengthen and add to their qualities.

ACRYLIC FIBERS: du Font's ORLON (1950); ZEFRAN by Dow Chemical; ACRILAN & CRESLAN by American Cyanamid Company.

The manufacturing process is similar to the others except for the chemical components from which they are derived. Although they all (man-made fibers) come from the same basic ingredients, the acrylic adds one more source from which it gathers its chemicals and that is limestone.

Acrylic fibers can be made into either of two shapes—fine, soft and luxurious to the feel or bulky similar to wool.

They are lightweight, resilient, durable and strong. They resist sunlight, heavy odors and chemicals. Acrylics are non-allergenic, mothproof, moisture and weather resistant, and are nonabsorbent.

Acrylics are widely used in textile industry including carpeting.

OLEFIN: (polyethylene) (polypropylene). Was introduced in the early 1960's although research was done as early as 1873 under the name of "Isobutylene." It get^4ts chemicals from some of the same sources as the others but more so from propylene and ethylene gases.

The fiber manufacture is similar to the others. Its fiber is abrasion resistant and is good in carpets that are placed in high traffic areas.

Herculon (tm) An extremely strong fiber, abrasive resistant, easy to clean and wears like iron. It is used a lot in furniture coverings and commercial carpets but is not now widely used in household carpets. It was available for homes a few years back but for some reason now it can't be found.

HOW ARE TODAY'S CARPET MADE?

After the yarn has been spun and wound onto spools, they are taken to the tufting machine. This machine is one that will make the part of the carpet that is so familiar to us all—the pile.

This is done by joining hundreds of spools of yarn together with the yarn ends being fed into needles (as many as a thousand). These needles are set-up on a long bar approximately \Y wide. They are all electrically controlled and in today's modern mills are connected to memory units or computers to weave whatever style and density the operator wishes to make.

As the yarn is then fed into these needles, it is punched through a large sheet of fabric, very similar to work done with a sewing machine as it makes its stitch, only with a thousand needles going all at once in a long line.

This large sheet of fabric is called the primary backing of your carpet and if you look down through the pile side of any carpet, that is what you'll see. This primary backing is fed into the needles as the machine is operating.

The type of carpet and style is all being determined at this stage. The yarn being fed into the needles will determine if it will be a frieze, a shag or a plush. Yarns are twisted differently for the various uses that will be required of them. The mechanical and electrical adjustments on the needles will determine the density of the carpet. The less expensive will have the needles punch the yarn at further distances from the previous punch. Each tuft could be placed as far apart as 1/2 inch which is often found with shags. Or with the more expensive carpets, for instance, the plushes could be as close as 1/8 inch. After the basic loop has been tufted into the carpet by the needles, it (the loop) will be cut to form the style of the carpet or just left alone and making the carpet a level loop pile carpet which is very common today. All of this is done on this first machine called the TUFTING MACHINE.

If the yarns were not already dyed before tufting, then the entire carpet would be dyed. There are many ways in which carpets are dyed and all are effective and long lasting.

The next process of importance is attaching the secondary backing to the primary backing. This secondary backing is extremely important. It provides first a method by which the tufts are held into place so they cannot be pulled out; and next it gives the carpet strength and weight without which a carpet could not last long enough to be of any value. This backing is glued on and pressed together. There are also some other steps such as trimming and clipping, and a great many inspections throughout the entire manufacturing process.

Once all this has been done the carpet is rolled and stored at the mill until dealers call for that particular type, style or color. The rolls at the mills are sometimes 350 square yard rolls or 263 feet long. When a dealer needs a carpet only 120 square yards or 90 ft. long, the roll will be cut at the mill and the required amount would be sent to the dealer. These large rolls of carpeting are very heavy and are moved around with forklifts using long poles that are put into the center of the roll of carpet. When the carpet is cut, it is done on a large cutting table; and when the roll of carpet has been mechanically unrolled the desired length, then a cutting saw will cross over the width of the table making a clean straight cut. Both rolls of carpeting are then remeasured for indexing and the ordered roll is loaded onto a truck and sent to the dealer.

CARPET TYPES

NOTE: ALL CONSTRUCTIONS OF CARPETS have a variety of factors involved that will determine the ultimate cost. For instance: type of fiber, twist of yarn, density of tufts (how many places the yarn enters the primary backing within a given area), and secondary backing material.

LEVEL-LOOP: *The twisted yarn is tufted through the primary backing—in and out over the whole face of the carpet to be. The tops of all the loops are level with one another.*

This carpet is the easiest pattern of carpet to construct, so the cost will generally be lower than for all other types of tufted carpeting. This carpeting will usually be found in rental units or less expensive tract homes.

The weave is short and tight using a continuous yarn. If pulled, it will unravel the entire length of the carpet. These carpets wear well. However, they are not the easiest to clean because dirt will get trapped on the underside of the loops. Loose dirt is easily removed by vacuuming but the grimy type of dirt gets trapped.

HIGH-LOW LOOP PILE: The twisted yarn is tufted through the primary backing and according to a pre-programmed mechanical or electric device, the tufting needles mil make patterns of high and low loops all across the surface of the carpet.

This type of construction is also easy and inexpensive to make. These, too, will be found in rental units and tract homes. Their wearability is better than the level loop only in that it tends to hide dirty or worn areas better.

This is due to the visual effect of the patterns in the carpet pile.

The cleaning of these types are slightly more difficult because the small loops tend to concentrate dirt which will leave dark lines throughout the carpet as years go by.

SCULPTURED SHAG—CUT & LOOP AND ALL OF ITS VARIATIONS: This is done by the twisted yarn being tufted through the primary backing. As the loop is formed, it is then cut at the top of the loop and laid open. Because the smaller loops are lower than the larger ones, they do not get cut.

This process now incorporates three methods of carpet construction: the straight loop tuft—the mechanical or electrical device forcing a smaller, tight tuft into pre-set patterns—and a cutting device. The cost of this type of carpet is understandably going to rise.

Many multi-colored carpets are of this type construction.

Cleaning is easier because loops have been cut and dirt is not trapped so easily but the small loops will still pose a problem over the years.

PLUSH—PLUSH SHAG OR VELVET PLUSH: *The yarn of the plush is only slightly twisted and then tufted. The tips are slightly flared and smooth-sheared to make an even, smooth appearance on the face of the carpet.*

The cost of construction is higher because of the quantity of fabric that must be used. Wear will depend on fabric and density. **NOTE:** THE ABOVE PLUSHES AND THE SAXONY PLUSHES BELOW ARE YOUR TWO HIGHER-PRICED CARPETS FOR THE HOME.

PLUSH—SAXONY: *The Saxony plush is similar in all respects to the regular plush except that the yarn has a tighter twist on it.*

This carpet could be better used in a home with a good deal of traffic. The tightness of the twist in the yarn will enable it to withstand more abuse than the regular plush.

Both plushes are easy to clean, except where the pile length exceeds 1/2 inch. Once the pile length gets over that, cleaning becomes more difficult. This is because the suction from the vacuum will lose its effect and dirt will accumulate at the base of the yarn. Thick, long-piled carpets have a luxurious appearance, but make sure that they are in rooms that won't get dirty.

FRIEZE (PRONOUNCED "Fre'say"): *This carpet is tufted of a highly twisted yarn, in fact, so twisted that it begins to knot up and knurl.*

This carpet is very durable and may even be used in a light commercial capacity. It is easy to clean and maintain. Friezes are priced in all ranges and are considered a good all-around carpet for the active family.

SHAGS: *This carpet is also easy and inexpensive to make. By tufting large loops and then cutting Quite often the yarn used in the shags are two a three different colors interspersed with each other-this will hide dirt and wear areas well.*

Shags seem to be on their way out, but at one time they were the most popular type carpet around. Some of their problems stemmed from making the pile yarn too long. Therefore, it would become matted very easily. Also, the vacuum could not penetrate these long fibers which were leaning over. Most shags were easy to make and therefore inexpensive to buy.

As time went by, the shag did get shorter and vacuuming and cleaning became easier and more effective. As a matter of fact, some of the shags are the easiest of carpets to clean because all sides of every yam can be cleaned right down to the primary backing. But they still cannot hold up in traffic areas.

CUSHIONED-BACKED
CARPETING

Another type of carpeting you will run across other than the tufted carpet is the cushioned-backed carpeting. They are used more in kitchens, bathrooms, recreation rooms, offices, and the like. Today, these carpets seem to be losing popularity.

There are also regular carpets with the cushion built in. This foam cushion is much thicker than the other type of carpeting used in kitchens or bathrooms. Many do-it-yourselfers have success with it as it is easily installed. The carpet and pad are in one piece rather than two pieces and the cushion is usually a good quality foam. It is a very practical piece of carpeting with several advantages and a few disadvantages.

ADVANTAGES: (1) simple installation for the homeowner, No seaming is needed as the carpet fits right together. It can be stapled, nailed or glued to the floor. (Glue only around the perimeter and on the seams).

(2) It is easily cleaned as long as you don't use any heavy scrubbing machines which might rip the carpet loose.

DISADVANTAGES: (1) You can't save the padding, consequently you have to buy carpet and pad all over again when you replace it. This can be more expensive in the long run. (2) The perimeter has to be glued down. When you take it up, it leaves a mess on the floor to scrape up. If your floors are hardwood, they'll have to be refinished if you leave them bare. (3) If you drag furniture across it and it is not glued down all the way across the floor it will bubble or rip.

FLAMMABILITY: Many consumers are concerned about whether or not their carpet is very flammable and will cause their house to become more of an insurance risk. Usually it is quite the opposite.

All carpeting manufactured today in the United States is tested by a government standard for flammability of the fabric. Their testing methods are very scientific and the fabric must pass the test before it can be sold. The test is called the "Pill" test. Simply put, they drop a flaming substance or a combustible substance on an area of the carpet. Then they check the time it takes the flame to spread across the carpet against their standards. The fibers will usually melt but not catch fire.

Carpets manufactured in the United States are not considered a fire hazard in your home.

ELECTROSTATIC SHOCK
WHAT IS IT? It is the electric shock that most people experience

by walking across the carpet and touching something metal that is grounded. As you walk across the carpet without touching anything, you build up quite a charge of electricity within your own system. When you do touch something, you'll get a big jolt.

This has been a problem for years with carpeting including wool carpets.

If there is a lot of moisture in the air your chances of being shocked are slight. A dry static outside air will increase shock conditions. There are some ways to help alleviate this.

1. If your carpet does not have a built in anti-shock treatment, you can buy aerosol sprays which will temporarily reduce the static in your carpet. However, keep in mind that they are only temporary and because continuous use will leave a residue in the carpet which attracts dirt, it

will compound your cleaning problems.

2. Buy a room humidifier to use when the outside climate is dry. They are not expensive and are good to have in the house. They will put just enough moisture in the air to reduce the static so you don't get shocked. Also, if the outside air is cold and dry, the added moisture inside will make the house feel warmer. With a humidifier, you will actually find your carpets staying cleaner. The reason is that in dry conditions, the positively charged static electricity in the carpets draws the negatively charged dust particles right out of the air (opposites attract). Reducing the positive charge in the carpets with the humidifier reduces the attraction of dirt to the carpet.

3. Many carpet manufacturers weave anti-static fibers right in with the carpet yarns. The finest fiber for static control that we have been able to find is made by du Pont and is called "ANTRON III."™ A carbon fiber is put into the yarn and it reduces static electric shock to a minimum so you cannot feel it. Antron III™ is used by many different carpet manufacturers. If you see a carpet made with it, you know it is a high quality fabric.

4. Another product out today to reduce static electricity and which very few people seem to know about is the negative ionizer. These little units operate on very low voltage electricity and dispense negatively-charged ions into the room. They are very effective for reducing static air and claim to be beneficial to everyone, especially those with breathing problems. They are produced by several different manufacturers and usually can be obtained though a health food store or direct distributors.

5. Time itself will reduce shock. The older and more worn your carpet gets, the less shock there will be. So the problem isn't something you will have to live with for 20 years that is if you keep the carpet that long.

PART II
Purchase

SO YOU THINK YOU NEED CARPETING?

After you've looked over your carpeting and decided it is either too worn out to put up with any longer or you're just plain sick of the color, you might reflect on these points for a minute before you run out and buy something.

The average person in the United States only makes three major investments in his lifetime:

1. **A HOME.** Would you buy a home without investigating at length whether it is within your price range and is what your own personal desires require?

2. **AN AUTOMOBILE**. A lot of things are considered when buying an automobile like gas mileage, repair frequency, and whether it meets the family needs. People shop for weeks or months for the right automobile.

3. **CARPETING.** It's quite an undertaking to get a good piece of carpeting in your house for a good price. The unfortunate thing is that most people will make this expensive investment without knowing what they are looking for or what they need.

YOUR FIRST DECISION IS, "HOW MUCH CAN I AFFORD TO SPEND ON CARPETING?" Select an amount you can spend without going into debt; then allow an additional 20% just in case you find a very good bargain on a much finer quality carpet. Pay ALL CASH if possible. You can always BARGAIN with cash. If you have to finance or charge your purchase, you lose at least 75% of your bargaining power. Don't be afraid of bargaining with people over the price of things. Most of the independent businesses would rather have your sale at a lesser price than no sale at all.

If you are working with cash and you do find that bargain that is slightly more expensive than your cash on hand, go ahead and finance only that extra amount. The overall investment on a quality carpet far out weighs the inconvenience of a small monthly payment.

A word of caution on financing and carpet. To carpet a house is rarely a necessity. In every incidence of a carpet purchase, it is either a convenience of a luxury. Both a home and automobile are vital, but not a carpet. So please don't extend yourself into debt for more than 90 days on carpet. Of course I'm not trying to tell you how to run your financial affairs. It's just that credit has been made so available today to the home owner, that more and more people are becoming totally overwhelmed by their indebtedness. Easy credit is a trap, so please beware.

Once you've determined what you can spend on the carpet, you now have to determine the COLOR. Home decoration is not to be made a complicated subject. It basically means living in the atmosphere and surrounding that makes you feel comfortable; what you like to have. But beware of certain things such as wild colors, ultra-modern furniture, and no-color harmony in the home, and trying to please other people with your home rather than yourself. You will be unhappy with your home after a very short while—finding yourself irritable and uneasy—if you allow other people to bring in things such as wild contrasting color schemes that you can't really live with. Try to stay with your nature colors and keep your carpeting harmonious throughout. You may want to make it more comfortable by adding a thicker or more firm pad.

The carpets that go down today are expected to stay down 5 to 7 years. It isn't that the carpets wear out in that short time but people, for some reason, get tired of looking at the same floor covering.

Pick out several colors that you can live with and narrow them down to one or two. HOW DO YOU DETERMINE THE COLORS YOU WILL NEED? Certain things in your home are predominant like furniture which harmonizes with other colors attractively. If you have a white or light-colored couch and you want to set it off with carpeting, you will not choose a white or light-colored carpet to set off a light-colored couch. We recommend natural colors—browns, greens, beiges— those you see in nature, especially for the floors.

Another way to determine the color your carpeting should be—this may sound ridiculous but it really is important—is to go outside and find out what color the DIRT is in the front yard or backyard. If it has a reddish color to it, then you will want a red-tinted color carpet (possibly a light brown). If it's a black rich dirt, then a darker tint—a multi color—would be good for this. If you have asphalt around your house (the driveway, etc.) and you walk directly from the asphalt onto your carpeting, you would want to look for a multi-color carpeting with some dark tones in it. A light dusty color dirt—desert sand or light clay—calls for shades darker than beige in the carpet.

So the rule of thumb is match the color carpeting with the color of dirt outside.

HOW MUCH LONGER DO YOU PLAN TO LIVE IN THE HOUSE? This is a definite consideration before you buy. If you plan to be there two years or less, go to a cheaper grade of carpeting, something that will hold up that long and still look good when you sell the house.

DAD WANTS BROWN FOR HIS DEN, MOTHER WANTS GREEN FOR THE LIVING ROOM, JOHNNY WANTS BLUE FOR HIS ROOM AND SUZIE WANTS RED FOR HER BEDROOM. WHAT DO I DO???

Many people carpet their homes in several different colors and styles. If you decide to do this also, let me say just a couple of things first.

1. The same carpet (style and color) that goes throughout the entire house, will tend to draw the house together into a single unit. Being harmonious, as a whole, it has a physiological effect on the family members drawing everyone together. Their house is one, their family unit is one.

   If a house has different carpets in each room, it tends to have physiological effect of confusion, anxiety and disharmony in the family unit.

2. The resale value of a house is lowered in the mind of a potential buyer if he walks into a house that has many different colored carpets. Because more than likely he will want to replace it all rather than live with the personality of the sellers family staring him in the face thru the carpets.

   If it is just one carpet throughout and if its clean, the buyer will not be so likely to have a conflict with it, and be more willing to give you the price you're asking for your home.

COLOR COORDINATE YOUR CARPET ACCORDING TO THE TRAFFIC IN YOUR HOUSE. To help you determine what kind of traffic you have, listed below are five types of traffic most commonly found with recommendations on types of carpet colors to use or stay away from.

1. Category I: Light traffic, no pets, no kids. The field is wide open. Choose any colors you like. This is the ideal solution for someone who can afford quality carpeting and not have to worry about wearing it out.

2. Category II: Light traffic, well-trained pets, occasional child or so (possibly grandchildren). Stay away from whites, off-whites, baby blues (in solid colors). Also not recommended are solid light yellows, pinks or wine colors.

3. Category III: Medium traffic, no pets, no kids. Most young married couples who have an active life together in the home fall in this category. AVOID all colors in Category II plus solid reds, blues, and yellows. GO with tweeds or multi-colors. The only solid colors that work here are the darker natural colors.

4. Category IV: Medium traffic, well-trained pets, 1 or 2 kids on occasion. Eliminate all the colors in Categories I through III (except multi-colors and darker natural colors) and shag carpeting (any long pile carpeting).

5. Category V: Average household traffic, trained pets, children. This is the category most of us fall into. There are family get-togethers and occasional parties. In other words, the house is really lived in. Stay away from all the above plus no pile length over 3/4", preferably 1/2", in height, and all light colors period. No expensive carpeting here. Stay in the medium price range, even into the lows. The medium price range is $9 to $14 at the time of this writing; the low range is $5.50 to $8.99. Anything lower is hard to find and shouldn't be considered for the average household use. These are used for rentals and fixer-uppers, etc.

Keep in mind the overall purpose of the carpet: Appearance, comfort, and investment value. When deciding on colors, remember that dark colors tend to shrink the size of the room in appearance while the lighter colors broaden the size of the room in appearance. Make note of how much natural light you have in the room. If your house is dark because of the direction it faces the sun or lack of windows, then select a floor covering that will illuminate the light you have. You would not choose white or lights if they are not suitable for your traffic use but you do want something that is not dark. With a lot of light in the house you will be more comfortable if you darken up the floors.

Don't allow the salesperson in the carpet store to help you decide what color you should have in your house. The overzealous carpet salesman will freely advise what HE THINKS you should have. Our research has discovered a lot of unhappy consumers who have made this mistake. By basing your decision on what turns him on, you may buy the color he selects and discover later the color is all wrong for YOU after you have paid for it. Then all you have is somebody to blame and a continual personality clash with the color.

In your selection of color(s), make up your OWN mind on the color suitable for YOU. This way you can only blame yourself and not the salesman, in the event of a mistake.

If you are an average family, don't try too hard to color coordinate all of your furnishings. The carpeting is the MAIN FEATURE of the home—the very first thing that people see when they walk in the door. If the carpeting is luxurious and beautiful, you can have just about any kind of furniture sitting around and it wouldn't make any difference. But if you have nice furniture and your floor covering has an odor or is worn out or dirty, it reduces the esthetic appearance of the home. It is important to keep the carpet well maintained and looking nice.

The wall-to-wall carpet seems to draw the entire house together—all the rooms and furnishings—and makes the house itself one complete unit rather than four walls and scattered pieces of furnishings all over.

ROOMS FOR SPECIAL THOUGHT

Now although for most homes one carpet throughout is not only the most appealing, practical and, as discussed earlier, will increase the selling power of a home. However, some homes need to have a special consideration, regarding those rooms that will be used for special purposes.

The recreation room is a special consideration. Usually a family will spend many hours together either watching television or playing games in this room. In fact if your house has a recreation room, it probably is the most used room of all. So by all means put down a good commercial carpet here. Sewing Rm.:Many housewives who have the time to sew, enjoy having a separate room set aside just for that purpose. Ideally the hard surface sheet vinyl would be perfect. But most ladies want something cozier, warmer and more comfortable, so sheet vinyl is out and carpet is in. Where the problem lies is in what kind of a carpet. So often I've been in a room that was used as a sewing room and the carpet was saturated with pins and needles. They are not easily removed and when stepped on sure hurt. The kids get stuck, and they will even penetrate the soles of your shoes. When you try to vacuum them up they just get stuck somewhere in your machine. These little needles get lost real easily in a carpet that is of thick pile (plushes, shags, etc.). So also do buttons. It's so frustrating to be putting on a button, and it drops out of your hand, or off the machine into a shag carpet. Especially when it's the only button on the kids shirt. You might find it, then again you might not. Our recommendation is that your consider a short pile commercial grade carpet. The weave is tight so the chances of losing even a straight pin are remote.

Another room for thought would be the hobby room. Again, if carpeting is all you'll settle for then so be it. Get an inexpensive indoor outdoor carpet. Don't glue it down!! Just have it cut to fit and have the door way anchored down with the same type of metal that is found where your carpeting meets hard floors. Around the perimeter of your hobby room floor you can anchor the carpet down with 2 sided tape, that any hardware store should have. This indoor outdoor carpet is very durable and can take nearly any kind of abuse. It can be quite inexpensive if purchased at a hardware or variety store. Lumber stores also have it on sale. At the time of this writing it can be purchased as cheaply as $1.99 per square yard to $3.99 per square yard. Most carpet stores have this available also but they usually carry higher quality goods and of course are more expensive. For hobby rooms your best investment is this cheaper stuff. When it gets worn out or so stained and soiled you can't stand it, just rip it up and throw it away and go buy some more. It's even easy to put down yourself.

CAUTION: If you are going to carpet your house, and a hobby room is being used by you, make certain to purchase enough carpet to also cover that hobby room. When it comes time to sell your home, you can then rip out that indoor outdoor carpet and install the carpeting you have for that room. Very few home buyers will use your home the same way you did. Also if you were to leave that hobby room floor with indoor outdoor on the floor it would lower the selling value of your house.

NOTE: When storing carpeting be certain to have the carpet rolled on a cardboard core, wrapped in plastic and kept off the floor at least by 3 inches. Your carpet dealer can arrange for it to be wrapped. Keep the carpet stored inside out of any weather. The best place would be the rafters in the garage, but don't allow it to hang from ropes or to be suspended on boards. Make certain that the roll of carpet is placed on a flat surface. Suspension from ropes or boards over a long period of time will tend to pull the fabric out of shape and when the carpet is installed you have bubbles that cannot be stretched out.

One other room would be the den or office, so many people today have to have an office in their home, just to keep records for tax purposes, much less any other business they may have. This room can have almost anything on the floor and be just what is needed, except the thick piled carpet. How many times have paper clips, or thumb tacks been lost to the carpeting. Also, the rolling back and forth of the desk chair must be considered. This can be handled by the plastic desk mat. Sheet vinyl might be considered, but there's just something wrong about having it in a den, even though it will meet all requirements. Commercial carpeting may add warmth. Ceramic would be too cold. Our suggestion for a den or home office would be hardwood parquet, with maybe an oriental carpet to set it off. It would give warmth, luxury, and practicality. If parquet is for you, be certain to take all furniture that may be moved, including the desk chair and have the bottoms of the legs tipped with plastic or hard rubber furniture caps. This will protect the floor from unnecessary scratches. The parquet floor today will, if used in taste, increase the sales potential of your home greatly.

WHAT ABOUT CARPETING THE KITCHEN, BATH-ROOMS, AND LAUNDRY ROOM?

KITCHEN CARPET is never ever clean except maybe the first day it is installed. As soon as you start cooking, the grease and food odors go into the air. Aside from landing on your cupboards, counters and ceiling, this grease also lands on your floor. You can scrub every part of your kitchen to get the grease up except on the carpeted floor.

The grease buildup in most kitchens at first is unnoticeable but in a few days you feel the stickiness of grease and food on cabinets and refrigerators. You can be sure this same stickiness is on your carpet and it is not easily removed. You first start seeing it when the doorway area leading from your kitchen starts getting darker and won't vacuum out. After one or two years, your shoes even start sticking to the floor in the kitchen.

Kitchen carpet, in our opinion, is nothing more than a grease-catching and grease-accumlating mat.

BATHROOM CARPETING is equally as troublesome and we advise against it. Toilets sooner or later overflow and who knows what's coming up with it. Getting out of the tub dripping wet won't hurt anything if you do it on occasion but some people like to bathe once a day and too much water in a closed carpeted room will lead to bad odors and eventual breakdown of the carpet. If it's on a wood subfloor, the water will cause the floor to warp. However, if you really want wall-to-wall carpeting in your bathroom, buy the latex rubber-backed carpeting designed specifically for bathroom use. The very fine soft material is the same as in the bathroom throw rugs and mats. You can cut this carpeting with scissors and install it yourself. The instructions are easy to follow. The neatest thing about this particular carpet is that when it does get dirty, soiled or soaked, you can just pick it up and wash it. It can be washed many times and will last up to 5 years. In our estimation, it is a worthwhile investment if you

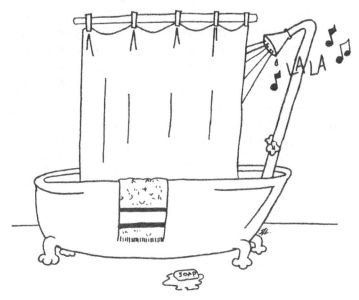

want wall-to-wall carpeting. Still, the most practical is the bath and toilet bowl mats that you can buy. They are very inexpensive and serve the purpose.

CARPETING IN LAUNDRY ROOMS is not recommended. Most laundry rooms are hard enough to clean as it is. With carpeting on the floor, it is very hard to get up the spilled detergents. A water leak is certain to happen sooner or later. Water and spilled detergent on the carpet only makes for a soapy, messy floor and you will forever have a filthy laundry room because of the residual detergent left in the carpet.

CARPET SQUARES

Carpet pile squares are not new. They have been used for years and are still in use today in commercial buildings. They are not cheaper— just more practical. They are glued in place. In an area of high traffic or abuse, if somebody should drop a cigarette and burn it, rather than having to replace the whole carpet, they just replace one square at a time. The Europeans have used this method in their homes for many years.

If you have carpet squares in your living room glued down and if you find an area that is wearing more than the other, simply pick up the squares and place them someplace where the wear doesn't show like under a couch or chair. The Europeans do this, there are some American firms that produce carpet squares, and it is becoming more popular.

An ADVANTAGE is the inexpensiveness of replacing worn out or damaged pieces of carpet. The overall cost is more expensive but if you buy more than you need for future repairs, the carpet will generally outlast any wall to wall carpeting if it is of commercial quality.

A DISADVANTAGE is that some of the carpet squares do not have good adhesive backing. The poor ones come up easily when cleaning.

CARPET THE WALL

If you're tired of looking at plain walls and the usual wall decoration such as pictures, clocks, mirrors, etc., are boring you, maybe you should consider carpeting a couple of your walls.

Don't be shocked! More people are doing it and it's not such a bad idea. It adds a distinctive appearance to any room. It makes an excellent soundproofing—a desirable feature for townhouses and apartments. If your room has a problem with too much light, try a dark carpet on the wall. It will dull the light plus add warmth.

A carpeted wall is as easy to maintain as a regular wall, maybe-even easier. Cleaning is simple. Just have the carpet cleaner do it when he does your floor carpet or you can do it yourself with an upholstery tool attachment that can be rented with the carpet cleaning machine.

Don't carpet a wall if there is a regular smoker in the house. The odor will build up in the carpet.

SPECIAL CARPET
DYE ORDERS

One very nice benefit that some carpet dealers can get for you is special color matches for your existing carpets. This can be a great money saver for folks who have perfectly good carpeting in their bedrooms, but the living room, dining room and hall, for instance, have to be replaced. After you have selected the type of carpet you want, the dealer will send a man out to get a sample of the carpet in your bedroom that you would like matched up with the new carpet. The dealer will then send to the carpet mill that piece of carpet along with your order. This does require more time and money to fill an order like this, but it is nowhere near as much money as if you had to replace the carpet in the bedrooms also.

MEASUREMENTS

The next thing is to get a rough measurement of the area to be carpeted. Measure in feet the width and length of each area. Multiply the length times the width of each area. (Be sure to include hallways and closets). Now add them all up and divide the total by 9. This will give you square yards. You will need *more* carpeting than what you have measured because carpeting comes in 12 foot rolls and it must all be rolled in *one* direction with as few seams as possible. Add 6% to your measurements for this. This will give you a closer estimate of the actual carpet you will need. It may even be a little over, but it is better for *you* to over-estimate than underestimate.

EXAMPLE:

Liv. Rm.	14 x 18 = 252 sq. ft.
Din. Rm.	8 x 10 = 80
Hall	4.5 x 12 = 54
Mst. Bdrm.	14 x 12 = 168
1 Bdrm.	12 x 10 = 120
2 Bdrm.	12 x 10 = 120

794 sp. ft.

Divide the 794 sq. ft. by 9 to find the total amount of sq. yards. You should have approximately 88.22 sq. yards. Now add 6% which is 5.29 sp. yards. This will give you a total of 93.51 sq. yds.

Double check the measurements. When it comes time for the salesman or the estimator to come out and measure your carpets, you will have something to gauge his estimate by. If his estimate is way under or over your figures, ask him how he got his measurements. Check it out yourself. Don't feel intimidated because he appears to be an expert.

If he's way over, call another dealer in and see what he comes up with but don't tell him what the first person said. Let him come up with his own figures.

It's unfortunate, but true, that some dealers or dealerships will bid high on the job if they think they can get away with it. They'll bid more yards than you're going to need for several reasons: (1) they're trying to cheat you out of more money than

You need to spend; (2) they gain from it by reselling the extra carpeting; or (3) a larger volume gives them a lower purchase price although you are charged the higher price.

CARPET WEIGHTS

Carpeting will sometimes be advertised with their weights listed. For instance, a 30-oz. pile weight might be mentioned. What does this mean?

Whenever any type of scale is used, it is to be a point of reference so that if you are looking for a denser carpet and you see a 20-oz. carpet, you will know that the 30-oz. carpet is more dense.

This ounce figure is calculated on the weight of the *pile only* in 1 square yard of that particular piece of carpet. If you had a piece of carpet 3' x 3' (1 sq. yd.) and you shaved off or pulled out all the pile fibers and put them on a scale, they would weigh 20 or 30 ounces or whatever the pile weight was figured at.

WHAT IS "DENIER?"

This is a term you will be confronted with as you shop for carpeting. It simply means "the unit of weight to express the fineness of the filament itself." In other words, when the filament denier number is low, that means the filament is very fine. So if you run across a carpet that has, for example, a 10 denier filament, then it is going to feel very fine and silky.

Both the pile weight and Denier are not used by every salesperson and it is not always available even from the mill. So while out shopping it may be impossible to compare one carpet with another based on these two weights. See section (Shopping Prices) for the best way of comparison.

REMNANTS: Not everybody will be able to carpet their entire home all at once. So after installing carpet in the main rooms (liv. din. hall) its decided to carpet the extra rooms later with remnants as it becomes possible to do so.

Buying remnants is much like buying your regular carpet, except that you can get a bad deal, much easier. Remember that the remnant should be a sale priced item, selling for less than a comparable carpet ordered from the mill. Most people never stop to question if the remnant they're buying is really cheaper and just buy on impulse. They see that big red tag on the roll saying "SPECIAL" or "SALE", and off to the cash register they go. Please check the prices of stores regular stock first, you may very well be able to save some money with price comparison. Where do remnants come from? There are 3 main sources. One is the obvious. If the store you're doing business with, stocks rolls of carpet, either on the floor or in a warehouse, that will provide many remnants. If for instance a customer before you need 120 yds. of carpet which would be taken out of a roll of carpet that was 135 yds. The store now has a 15 yd. remnant, just right for a master bedroom for you.

The second source of remnants is the carpet mill itself. Quite often a store owner can go to the mill and buy a truck load of remnants.

Now the third way a remnant comes into existence is actually quite common among the unscrupulous carpet dealer. It happens like this. The carpet dealer comes out to measure your house for carpet and finds that it will take 120 yards. But he suspects that you have no idea of how much you may really need so he adds 12 to 15 yds. to his actual estimate. So he now estimates your house for 135 yds.. When the carpet is delivered to the store, that 15 yds. is cut off, rolled up and sold as a remnant. So you not only have to pay for your own carpet but his extra 15 yds. also, along with the extra tax freight, and labor. On an expensive carpet the amount lost to a swindle could be as much as $400.00 just for those 15 yds.. Bear in mind that the dealer now turns around and sells the carpet, you paid for, again. Sounds unbelievable doesn't it? Many dealerships do this including even some estimators for large dept. stores. The above happens more often that anyone would care to guess, and the only way to avoid this is to get educated in the field yourself and shop around, with scrutiny.

SECONDS: Seconds are carpets that have been rejected by the mill for one reason or another. Quite often the defect in the carpet is very minor and is hardly noticeable. This makes an opportunity for you (if you know of a dealer who sells seconds) to get a decent carpet at a much reduced price. But again, compare the goods with the regular stock.

USED CARPET: As a general rule, the used carpet is not such a good idea unless that's all you can afford. However, there are occasions that people offer their old carpet for sale and it is still in decent condition. If you should be in the market for this, may I point out some things to look for: 1. Odor-if there is an odor of urine, do yourself a favor and pass this opportunity up. 2. Stiff or flaking secondary backing— If the carpet backing is not flexible or cracks when you bend it, the carpet for all practical purposed, is impossible to install properly. 3. Fleas or animal hair— although the presence of fleas and hair, does not dictate the carpet condition, its a good indicator of carpet use. Should you decide to buy used carpet, make certain to unroll it entirely and smell it carefully in many spots. You may install it yourself but if you plan to have a professional install it, keep in mind that, he will charge you more for a used carpet than for a new one. The reasons are that used carpet is much harder to install and work with. Its usually dirty and many times requires more seams than the new carpet does.

THE HIGH PRESSURE
SALESPERSON

No matter what kind of carpet store you go to, you may run into the high pressure salesperson. They usually work on commission. The higher the sale, the more money they make for themselves. Their commission is based on the amount of carpeting sold so be on guard! Don't be in a hurry to buy! You don't need to be in a rush to spend a lot of money. Let it sit in the bank and draw interest for a little longer while you shop around.

Salespeople earn their money with their mouth so they've had lots of training on how to flatter you. We have had them walk into our house when it was a total disaster and with a big smile on their face say, "My, what a lovely home you have." Believe me, they can lie through their teeth and never blink an eye. They've taken college courses on how to be motivated to sell. They've gone to seminars on how to influence people. The salesperson has books upon books on how to sell. A good salesperson can sell just about anything to anybody and come out smelling like a rose. They are geared for only one primary purpose—to enrich and enhance themselves. The customer is only considered as a means by which the salesperson can gain more.

In spite of all this, there is always the exception—the salesperson who really has your best interest in mind first. If there were more caring salespeople in the world, books like this would not even be needed because the information would be volunteered and given to you. But as life would have it, it just "isn't" so!

Many salespeople in the floor covering industry are the same as those in all other fields. They know how to sell but not much about what they're selling. This manual is designed to give you enough ammunition to protect yourself by being informed on the subject rather than at the mercy of the unscrupulous or unknowledgeable. Floor covering involves so much from the first stages of manufacture to the maintenance and cleaning that there are just not that many people around who have been involved with it at all. Usually, salespeople in the carpet business have never installed a carpet or cleaned one (or had to repair one). This fact alone leaves most sales people in the dark about what is really best for you. So they fake it. Let's hope that they too will read this book.

WHO DO YOU BUY FROM? WHAT STORES DO YOU GO TO?

The best reference always is from your friends and people you can trust. If you have two friends who have had floor coverings installed in the last year or two by the same dealership, and they can recommend him highly, then that's probably the place you're going to be dealing with. It is at least a good starting point and you will probably come back to them when you have shopped around.

Don't take your friends recommendations, though, if their carpet was installed six months ago or less. Floor covering should be down at least six months before you make a determination on the quality of installation and carpeting. In six months in the average home, it will have gone through most of the climate changes that were necessary, and through most of the wear and tear that will probably come upon it. It will not have gone through a major cleaning yet but you have to assume that if it's going to hold up under most of these conditions, it will hold up under cleaning.

Newspaper Ads are the next major source that people turn to in searching out carpet stores.

LET'S LOOK AT THOSE ADS! ARE YOU REALLY GOING TO SAVE?

Ads in the newspaper are to get you to come buy something and buy it right now because if you don't, you'll never get another chance like this again. "Yep, if you're not here to buy our special 'bargain' by 9 p.m., you will forever and eternally be sorry."

Do you ever look at those ads? They appear everyday in the newspaper.

Since we cannot analyze everybody's ads, we'll stick to the carpet sales and carpet cleaning ads and give you some pointers to keep in mind.

All advertisements are not bad. The general use of advertisements is to acquaint you with a product or service, either something new or useful. The problems come with the "Special Deal" ads. It's true you can

have a Special Deal and it truly is a Special but too often that Special Deal is to get you in their door or them in your door.

But in all fairness to the honest retailer, there really can be a bona fide "Sale," that is truly spectacular and honest in all respects.

An example of this might be illustrated in this experience I had: We were recently traveling in the South and were watching this television ad that sounded absurd. This one outfit was selling carpet for $2.99 per square yard that would normally sell for $8.95 per square yard. Now anybody would know that this sounds phony. In this particular instance, though, it was on the level. Apparently a local carpet store had gone bankrupt and had a tremendous amount of inventory in the store. In order to get at least something out of all that had been invested, the inventory was turned over to this other carpet store for liquidation. He sold all of that carpet store's inventory at far below the original cost of the goods. The liquidating store got a good commission plus advertising costs paid for by the bankrupt business. Also, everyone who came in to look at the very special sale items could have a chance to look over the regular stock and pick from that if they wanted to. As it was, the sale was a great success and the advertising retailer made out very well. So did the bankrupt dealer, by selling nearly all of his inventory and making some money on the side to boot. So some spectacular special sales are real and can save many dollars. But in reality these don't happen too often so don't expect them.

THE BARGAIN

This term has been so misused that it has lost its meaning. In the traditional mind, if you walked away with a Bargain, it meant that you did some bargaining to get it (horse trading or dickering). In other words, you got something of more value than what you had to give. Bargains were not an everyday occurrence.

Today, however, if you look at the ads, every-time you turn around you'll get a Bargain. Don't you believe it!

If you get a Bargain you are getting something for less than everybody else. The next time you see a Bargain Days ad someplace, hop in your car and go down to the store and try to get a Bargain. See if you come out paying less than the posted sale price—for anything!

What the ad really says is:

1. "We've made enough money selling the chair for $109. Now we'll sell it for $89. After all, we only paid $49."

2. "Come on in! We'll sell you this freezer for $349 which is our sale price. Our "regular price" was $379 but for the last year we sold it at $349."

3. "We have a factory clearance sale of dinette sets for $419. Our regular price was $399."

It's a shame but after digging into the advertising policies of some of the largest nation-wide retailers, these above examples were actual cases that happened. If you can't trust the big boys, why should you trust the little boys?

With floor covering ads, it's the same story:

1. THE FREE INSTALLATION: Don't ever believe this one. You're paying for every yard laid. It has all been calculated into the cost of the carpet you buy. Watch out here for those extra charges!

2. THE FREE PAD: Same as for the free installation. You pay for everything, except with the pad they are giving you the pad at cost. It's usually next to the poorest quality and if you want to upgrade, they charge you double the markup. The story goes something like this:

Customer: "How can you give away free padding when the dealer down the street has to sell it for a dollar a yard?"

Store Salesman: "Well, we don't have to pay for the pad ourselves. It's an advertising promotion from the mill. To sell their carpet, they will give the pad away."

Customer: "Wow!! What a Bargain. This must be my lucky day."

3. THE PRICE IS SLASHED SALE: "Our regular low price was $12.99 per yard (includes pad and installation), but for this next three days only, the price will be $8.99 which includes pad and installation.

This ad must be in every major newspaper in the country at least once a week. So let's look at it. First the price. If the cost from the mill were $8.99, then the markup would be 44 % - 45 % which is about right. But, you know they aren't selling it at cost. They have to make at least 60$ per yard on the carpet plus 20$ per yard on the pad plus another 20$ per yard on the installation—totalling at least $1 a yard on the cost. They can't stay in business unless they average at least $1 per yard sold.

This ad tells you something right away about whom you're dealing with. Just last week he was getting $5 profit on the yard, so why is he willing to cut $4 profit off this week? Ads have a special effect on people. If you read an ad in the newspaper week after week from the same dealer, then your mind starts thinking that this guy is always offering you a good deal. So who do you go and see when it is time to buy? Him, of course!

I'd like to especially emphasize here that all merchants that advertise are not greedy and deceptive. There are many honest businessmen who advertise just to let you know that they are there too. There are also many honest salespeople who are sincerely interested in you and do all in their power to make you the best deal so that you are happy.

4. THE GREAT PERCENTAGE OFF SALE!!! You've certainly seen the ads that say something like, "SAVE 30% - 50% ON OUR 'ALL ITEMS MUST GO' CLEARANCE SALE."

First, look at the positive side. It is true that dealers get overstocked. It is cheaper to sell at a profit reduction than it is to let the inventory sit and collect dust. This does happen when a dealer gets excited about a product and orders more than he should, only later to find out that nobody else got as excited as he did. He has to sell at a greater profit loss. NOTICE, I said profit loss, not by any means a "loss-loss," where he sells it cheaper than what he paid for it. This only happens in bankruptcy when all inventory has to be liquidated to pay off creditors.

So how can he offer 50% off sale? Let's take one yard of carpeting, for instance, that cost $8.95 a yard from the mill. The retailer adds a 45% markup to get his regular price of $12.98 a yard. This is the price that was on his shelf last week.

In this morning's newspaper he advertises 50% off the regular retail price which makes the price $6.49 a yard, right? That can't be. He's losing nearly $2 per yard on the sale. Even if we figure in his 5% cash discount offered him from the mill, he still can't buy that carpet for under $8.50 per yard. He maybe could get an additional 10% off by ordering 10 rolls from the mill. He still would have to pay $7.65 per yard.

How can he sell you carpet and pay out of his own pocket $1 for every yard you buy? He can't. His 50% sale price really isn't $6.49, but $10.96. You may say, "How can that be 50% off?" Legally it is. You see, it's 50% off from his profit margin. Remember, in the beginning he added his 45% markup to establish the retail price. He took 50% off that 45% markup or 22.5% and added that to the original price.

There is nothing legally wrong with this practice except it has a tendency to deceive the consumer into thinking he is getting something at half price.

Let's take one more example to show you how the retailer would have to make his regular retail price exorbitant in order to really give you 50% off. If he buys at $8.95, he would have to make over a 100% markup to make a profit on a 50% off retail price sale. Approximately 125% or $11.19 added per yard makes his regular price $20.14 per yard. Now, as advertised, deducting the 50% off gives you a sale price of $10.07 which would be a bargain. If you can get carpeting for around $1 a yard above cost, you are doing well.

The question is, "If the retailer should jack his prices up through the sky on a regular basis, then is he a very greedy person and should not be trusted in the first place??"

ADS DEALING WITH CARPET CLEANERS are in Part II under *"Carpet Cleaning Advertisements. "*

SHOPPING PRICES

Select 4 different carpet outlets at which to shop prices. This will be a full day's project but try for all 4 stores in one day so that your mind is fresh from one store to the next. You may not think that you can take this much time but the amount of money you are investing requires it. Do it on a day off or a weekend with your spouse or friend. Make it a fun day and go out for dinner that night and talk over what you've discovered. This way you won't be disturbed by outside influences and can keep your mind on the subject until it is done.

A very important note at this time. Because of manufacturing cost, carpet prices are going up constantly. From one month to the next the price may change as much as 20%. So, when you do go out to shop, try to get it all done in a period of a few days, because what may be quoted you as the price this month may well be higher next month. The dealer has no other option but to pass higher costs he has to pay the carpet mills on to you. If you feel that it will take you several

weeks to make up your mind, ask the dealer if he has been notified of a pending price rise. Most mills will give a 15-30 day advanced warning of future price increases.

When you go to a dealership there are two prices that you work with in determining how much you pay—the "cut" price and the "roll" price. The ^cut" price is any amount of carpeting under 100 yards. There may be a few exceptions but this is the general rule. If you buy the cut amount or less than 100 yards, then you will probably pay more money than if you bought more than 100 yards. It's a price break because of the quantity of carpeting you are buying.

The "roll" price is based on a roll of carpet more than 100 yards. The price variation between the two is as much as 90C on the yard. However, don't go out and buy 100 yards if you only need 90 yards. If you need 97 yards it might pay you to check out the roll price to see if it is cheaper to buy 100 yards.

In the very first store you visit, you should be able to determine which carpeting is going to look the best on your floor. WHICH STYLE (NOT COLOR) DO YOU WANT ON YOUR FLOOR? Level loop? Plush? Shag?

Compare styles with like styles. A shag with a shag. A plush with a plush. A level loop with a level loop. You can't compare a Mercedes with a Ford and say you're gong to buy the Ford because it's a better bargain. Or even a Pinto with a Thunderbird and take the Pinto as the best deal because of price. So compare STYLE FOR STYLE.

Take a note pad. Make notes on the sample you select. Look at the back side of the sample. There are things to look for: the kind of nylon used, guarantees, and the backing itself. Two basic types of backing are used today. They are both good but one is more tested than the other. The jute backing has been used for many years and has stood the test of time. However, it does have certain qualities which you may not want in your carpeting. One is that moisture in hot, humid areas will cause it to shrink or bubble up. This is characteristic of jute. It can be eliminated with a good stretch on the carpet. Still, jute has been used for years and is definitely a proven backing.

We feel there is a better backing out today. It does cost more but is worth it. It is the polypropylene-backed carpet or the "ActionBac"™

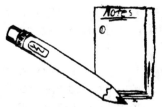

carpet. It's an entirely synthetic backing without any natural fiber in it. It eliminates undue stretching or shrinking and the problem with mildew as it is moisture resistant. There is one thing you want to look for with the synthetic backing and it is easy to spot: the squared-off little formations of fiber strands rather than a mish-mash like you have on the jute backing. The samples will say if it is "ActionBac"™ or has a similar poly back on it.

Turn the sample itself over and check the pile or the top part of the carpet. Look for several things here:

1. The density of the fiber. A good way to do this is bend the whole sample over the edge of table and look all the way down to the backing. If you see a lot of space in between the woven strands, it is a lesser quality carpet. The closer together the strands are woven, the denser the carpet. The denser the carpet, the higher the quality.

2. The feel and appearance of the yarn. Is there a lustre to it? If the yarn is dull, make note of it. If it has a sheen or shine to it, make note of it. See what you want to have in your home.

3. Is it a twisted yarn? For instance, the plushes (the Saxony plushes) have a twist and you want to compare that count. Take one yarn and count how many twists are on it. Five to six twists to the 1/2" indicates good quality.

All this may sound like a hassle but it's better to go through a few hours of hassle to get what you want and need than it is to make a mistake or trust someone else's decision. Too many people today in America want others to make decisions for them. They live their whole life letting other people make up their minds for them. This may be good in some small areas but when it comes to large financial investments, it is best that you make your own decisions and take responsibility for your own actions.

CARPET GUARANTEES

As mentioned, the guarantees should be on the back of the samples in the store. Listen to what the salesperson says. If he tells you there is a guarantee, get it in writing when you're ready to buy. AS-SUME NOTHING! The textile manufacturer's guarantees state in writing how long they think your carpet will last or how much the carpet will wear in a certain period of time, usually 5 years. These guarantees are valid and honored by the companies who write them.

But be absolutely certain to read them carefully. If you have any questions, ask the salesperson to explain it to you. The reason for this is that before the guarantee is honored there are certain conditions that must be met, such as:

1. That particular carpet can only be used in the home;
2. Must be installed by professionals using only acceptable installation techniques and materials; and
3. Stairways are excluded.

You'll probably never need the guarantee but having it shows the carpet is better than the ones without it.

WALK OUT OF STORE #1 after you have seen styles, general colors and prices. Whatever you do, don't let the salespeople talk you into coming to your house to measure "just to give you a free estimate." If they come out before you are ready, even though you may not think so, it actually does kind of obligate your mind to see them go through the trouble of coming out and measuring. It is a very troublesome thing for them to do. Estimating a house is really quite a talent. A lot of mistakes are made in it all the time due to inexperienced and untrained people so don't bother them for an estimate at this time. They may well be the ones to install your carpet later. Know for yourself that you are doing the right thing.

GO to at least 3 other stores. In selecting which stores to go to, pick out 1 large department store, 1 large franchise carpet outlet, and 2 independent retailers. For this you need a little background information on these three major carpet outlets and advantages and disadvantages to going to each one.

1. THE LARGE DEPARTMENT STORE CHAIN. They buy carpets in train-load lots and deliver to all their stores around the country. They have a few good points about them. One is you can finance it (upon approval)

on your credit card. Even if you don't have a credit card, if you're a potential big buy customer and you have a history of good credit, you can probably open up an account that day and secure the deal.

Another good point is that they guarantee the carpet. Most of these department stores have a fine reputation for making certain that if there is anything at all wrong with their product, they will replace it or refund your money. Those are two advantages you can count on in the department store chains.

There are some bad points. In spite of the possibility that they *could* sell their products cheaper, generally their prices are much more than other dealerships. Also the installation is more expensive. If you finance it at the current 18% (who knows where that is going to go?), you're paying even more money for the carpet.

You usually cannot bargain with them. Their prices are fixed. If there is any bargaining done in these stores it's only on the local management level and is very rare.

The department store chains put their own name brands on the samples and their carpets. They do not make this carpeting. They buy it from the same mills as everybody else and put their own names on them. Therefore, if you are a brand name shopper, you cannot determine who made the carpet. It isn't really necessary to know who made them if the department stores back up their product, but some people just like to know what mill made it and where it was made.

You should, of course, shop around. Sometimes dealerships have better offers than the department stores.

2. THE FRANCHISE CARPET STORE. This new concept in the chain store idea is moving up fast in the carpet industry. Their claim to fame in all their ads is basically the same as in the department store ads, "We buy these carpets in large quantities for a lower price and pass the

savings on to you." It's true they can do all these things but again, it is not very often that it's really the case.

One of the advantages of buying from this chain store is that they usually have a tremendous inventory on hand, even more than the local department store. It's ready to put in today. That appeals to the impulsive buyer. They look at whole rolls of carpeting and say, "I want this carpeting," and have it installed the next day.

These carpet outlets are very convenient and have everything under the sun in the way of floor covering. It's a one-stop shopping idea. You just stop in, get everything you want, and go home. It's a convenient way to shop—something Americans have been used to for sometime.

Generally they will offer a short-term financing program. Because it is short term you will pay less. If you cannot pay cash and have to finance, this is a good way to buy.

The disadvantages: Again, we'd like to emphasize the prices are really not that low. You can almost always get a better price at an independent dealer. The chain stores will very often put their own brand names on the carpet also, limiting your ability to know what you are getting and where it is from. You can bargain with them a little more than the department store but not much.

3. THE INDEPENDENT CARPET DEALER:

The major advantage here is that he is local and he has his name on the line. He doesn't want his name to get a bad reputation.

You can bargain with him. For the most part he will have many selections and styles and should be able to supply just about whatever you need. The owner, himself, is usually available and this a very good point to keep in mind. If you go to an independent dealer you can deal directly with the man in charge. If you go to anybody else but an independent, you're not dealing with anybody of any importance and if you win an argument with him, you haven't gained anything.

In the independent store you are somebody which gives just a little bit of dignity of being yourself. You're not just a number or just another customer to the independent dealer. He will do his best to please you as he wants your repeat business and your recommendations to friends.

There is only one real disadvantage to be considered with the independent dealer: he may go out of business without notice. Anybody can go out of business including the large chain stores. But the chances of the small independent business are so much greater these days, especially if it's honest. Your chances of getting burned by an honest, reputable independent dealer are, however, still minimal.

Shop the independent _store that has a good reputation and has been in the carpet field for at least 3 years, not necessarily a retailer but in the carpet field—either installation or cleaning. By then he has some sort of reputation that you can depend on and if he has lasted the last 3 years, there's a pretty good chance he'll last another 3 years. Your carpet guarantees only last 5 years and the installation guarantee 1 year.

4. THE DEALER WHO OPERATES FROM HIS HOME: Every large town has one or two people who sell carpeting from their home. They will advertise in the local paper that they can sell you carpetting much cheaper than the stores because their overhead is so low. This is a true statement but rarely is the case. On our examination of several people doing this in our area, we found that they were selling for just as much as the stores and in a couple of cases even more.

Now out of all the carpet outlets these will cause you the most problems. Many times these folks don't have business licenses or qualifications to perform the simplest business transaction. There is little you can do as a dissatisfied customer to get results. But to help balance out the scales, there are also honest business men operating a carpet store out of their homes, not many, but a few. If you should know personally of a man doing this, then go ahead and give him the benefit of the doubt. Let him bid on your job. But for your own safety, be sure that this man has been in business for a least a couple of years.

PADDING

As you shop and consider what kind of carpet to buy you must also consider the padding.

Padding was originally used to keep carpet from wearing on the back side. Today we can add a few more virtues to it. It increases the insulation capabilities of the floor covering up to 10%. It reduces noise level. It adds comfort to the feet. It helps the carpet stay in better shape. It makes vacuuming and cleaning your carpet much more effective. It can also make a less expensive piece of carpet have a more luxurious feel and appearance. It will increase the life expectancy of the carpet.

Padding comes in four categories:

1. Felt or jute (consists of jute and animal hair). It is manufactured in weights ranging from 40 to 56 oz. per sq. yard. This pad has been used for many years and has stood the test of time,

proving to be effective and still a reliable product.

It does have 2 disadvantages to the home owner. Although some what resilient it is not nearly as comfortable to walk on as the newer pads now available. Also, in the event of floods, it usually becomes necessary to replace the jute pad once it has been soaked.

2. Sponge Rubber (waffle), manufactured in 40 to 120 oz. per sq. yard. With 80—100 oz. range as the most popular with home-owners. This pad was the first major improvement made to padding and gave the person a soft cushion to walk on.

Here too is a product that has been tested by time and for all practi-cal purposes is a good product. The only disadvantage noted, is that in the event of excessive dirt working down through the carpet into the pad, the pad does begin to deteriorate.

3. Bonded Urethane (Rebond), manufactured in weights of 4 lb. to 8 lb., with 4.5—5 lb. being the most popular among homeown-ers. As the 2 types of pads listed above were measured by the weight of one sq. yard, this Rebond is calculated quite differ-ently. The measurement is determined by the weight of a cubic foot of this pad. In other words, if you were to buy a 5 lb. pad, you would know that 1'xl'xl' cube of that pad weighed 5 lbs.. This Rebond adds also a new factor to padding. Thickness, usu-ally coming in dimensions from 3/8" to 3/4" with the 1/2" and 9/16" being the most used by the homeowner. When choosing thickness you are considering comfort mainly, but if you are replacing the old pad with a newer and much thicker pad it may be necessary to have the bottom of your doors sawed off, so as to open and close them after the new carpet has been installed. Bonded Urethane is exactly what the name implies. Pieces and chunks of Urethane implies. Pieces and chunks of urethane foam are bonded together with heat and chemicals to form a blanket of padding. The finer that the pieces and chunks are ground up will determine the density and weight of the pad. Although a newer product than the previous two it has shown itself to be durable and effective in all respects. The price is competitive. Dirt and water have no effect on it, making it a good choice.

4. Prime Urethane foam (straight foam), manufactured in weights from 1.2 to 3 lbs.. With the 3 lb. being the most desirable for homes.

The thickness of the Prime Foam, would be the same as for the Rebonded Foam. Although the means of measuring weight is the same as rebond, the product is altogether different in that it is pure grade urethane (no imperfections).

The lowest grade and quality of the prime urethane pad is usually the type placed in the inexpensive homes, mobile homes and apartments. Or the type advertised as "Free Pad" with purchase. On the other hand the higher grade urethane, will be found as the most expensive and most desired pad of all.

DO YOU NEED PADDING?

If your old carpet is still down and you can't feel the hard floor through it, it's fairly safe to assume that new padding will not be necessary. Of course, you may want to have new padding if your old padding is not soft or comfortable to you. You can buy whatever you want but we are emphasizing necessities—buying new carpeting doesn't necessarily mean you *have to* buy new padding.

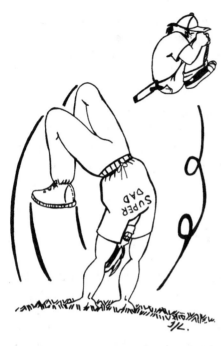

You may have an area of your floor that was soaked at one time because of an overflowing toilet or leaky roof, or whatever. This doesn't mean you have to replace all the padding in your house. If it was a jute or hair felt type padding, you should have to only replace the area that was soaked. If it was rebonded rubber and dried out well, you shouldn't have to replace it at all.

If an area of your floor is emitting mildew odors or a mustiness, it probably is caused from an overabundance of moisture that never dried properly (see Section on "ODORS & DEODORANTS"). That area will need new pad. If the carpeting has been abused from improper cleaning or by animals, you can pretty well figure on replacing the padding. What happens to the top of the carpet also happens to the pad.

SOIL RETARDANTS
SUCH AS SCOTCHGARDING

The soil retardants such as "Scotchgard"™ are placed in the fabric at the time of manufacture. This is the most thorough and complete method of putting in soil retardants and they are effective. However, it is good to keep in mind that this is a TEMPORARY protection and because it is a chemical covering that is placed over the fabric, it will break down with use and with cleaning. Once it is gone, it will never be replaced with the thoroughness as it was originally when the carpet was made. (For exception to this see Section on Nylon, page 9-ANSO IV)

WHAT ARE FOUNDATION "GRADE LEVELS"?

It is important to know your "Grade Levels" before you buy carpeting. Basement rooms are commonly known as "below grade"—the floor is below the grade level of the soil around you. Moisture from the soil will come up through a concrete slab floor, maybe not in water form, but in the form of alkalis and other chemical deposits on the top side on your concrete slab. It will always feel moist, damp and cold. This is due to the placement of the concrete slab or flooring below the grade level of the soil outside your house.

"On Grade" means that slab level or floor level of a concrete slab is at approximately the same height or level as the dirt outside. This very same moisture problem can happen with carpet installed "on grade."

"Above Grade", of course, means above soil level and you won't have a problem with moisture here.

When you buy carpeting for below grade or on grade levels, don't get a carpet that glues directly to the floor (like commercial or indoor/outdoor, etc.). The glue simply won't hold because the moisture will loosen the glue and it will come up. You have to go with a standard type installation where the carpet is stretched over the padding onto a tack strip.

NOW YOU CAN BARGAIN!

Once you've narrowed the choice down to 2 dealers (from the 4 stores you visited), you're now ready to go and start bargaining. Today in the 1980's, the average markup of carpeting for the average store can be anywhere from 10% to as high as 100% above the cost of the carpeting from the mill. So you have plenty of room to bargain with but keep one thing in mind: The store is only able to stay in business because of the profit that it makes. There are a lot of costs involved and you don't want to cheat the dealer out of his fair profit Profit is not a sinful thing or something to be ashamed of. It should be a fair profit to pay expenses and provide a decent living for the dealer. Inventory is expensive to maintain and even the samples have to be purchased at least 50% of the time. Other overhead expenses are rent, utilities, payroll, taxes, advertising, etc. All this comes out of the mark-up that he's making on the carpet.

Try not to get him down to a point where he is not comfortable. It you can get down to anywhere near the 35% above cost range, you can do quite well. There is no way to determine what that 35% range is except by bargaining with more than one dealer. Remember you're bargaining now with the very SAME TYPE of carpet with EACH dealer, not necessarily the same manufacturer but the same type of carpeting. You can get a pretty good idea of where you stand on this markup with the dealer if you're bargaining with at least one other dealership.

There are some dealerships that are below 35%. 35% above cost is the average starting point for markup on carpet. There are others that are much lower. We know of some that sell to the public at 10% across the board all the time. If you happen to find one and you know the installation is good, then you've really got yourself a good deal.

THE ACTUAL PURCHASE OF THE CARPET

Once you have decided upon what to purchase, there are certain things you should expect. You should expect to put at least 50% advance down on this purchase price and, in some cases, even the full material price. DO NOT PAY IN ADVANCE FOR THE LABOR. You may ask, "Why put an advance down payment on the purchase?"

Most carpet dealers have this situation happen to them over and over again: Somebody will order a carpet. The dealer in turn orders it from the mill, and that puts the responsibility on him to pay for it. The carpet may be 3 or 4 days down the order line and then the customer decides he doesn't want the carpet after all. He thinks he should just be able to cancel the order and not have to pay anything. This means the dealer has to pay out of his pocket either a restocking charge or a restocking charge and a delivery charge if the order has been shipped. It is an expensive loss and not just a few dollars that we are talking about. Once the order has been cut from the floor of the mill, the dealer has to pay. So when the dealer asks for money down, he is asking for a guarantee from you that you will bear the responsibility for your purchase.

If you order carpet from a mill in your part of the country, within two states away, you can expect delivery within one to four weeks. If you live near the mill you can expect it within 10 working days. Most often though, the carpet that you've chosen is manufactured in another part of the country altogether and delivery will take from 2 to 6 weeks.

Have the dealer confirm the delivery date from the mill or warehouse at the time you purchase. Then, for your own peace of mind and also for the dealer's peace of mind, allow at least one to two extra weeks beyond the time of delivery to have your carpet installed. If you are in a hurry we recommend that either you buy from the inventory that was on the sales floor or at best make sure you buy from the closest local mill. Your dealer can give you that information.

THE INSTALLATION OF THE CARPET—WHAT TO EXPECT

The day before installation, you have a lot of work to do. You should be ready for the installers when they arrive. Try to move every piece of furniture from all the areas of the floor to be covered. This is a major job and can involve a lot of headaches, but the men who install floor coverings are not paid furniture movers.

If they should accidentally break or scratch your furniture, they really cannot be held too responsible for it. These men do not mind helping people move furniture but it is not something that you should expect for the price of installation, unless it is agreed upon in advance. Many installers have to charge more money for moving furniture because of the time involved and their time is money. If they charge for it then they should carry a certain responsibility for the moving of your furniture.

It is much better to do it yourself and get some friends to help. Many times homeowners have found that moving the furniture gives them opportunity to dust and clean in areas they can't ordinarily reach and to rearrange their house in ways they have wanted to for a long time.

If you cannot move all the furniture yourself, take all the small furniture out: the lamps; the end tables; coffee table;. TV; stereo; empty the bookcases entirely and move the bookcases out; the closet floors cleaned out; get everything off the floor—magazines, newspapers, etc. Remove all drawers from dressers, hutches, etc. and take them out so the rest can be moved easier.

After you have removed all or part of the furniture, then vacuum your carpet thoroughly. The reason for this is that when the installers come and rip out the existing carpeting, there is going to be dust and dirt flying all over. You will never believe you had so much dirt and dust embedded in the carpet. A good job of vacuuming will minimize the dust considerably.

Two installers are usually required for an average household job. One

man can do one or two rooms though if that is all you are carpeting. They will lift out the old carpet and take it with them after they have finished the job. If they have to take it to the dump, they may have to charge you a small fee to haul it to the dump. If for some reason you want to keep the carpet, they will roll it up and place it aside for you.

If you're not sure what to do with the old carpeting here are some suggestions: You can sell it yourself. Cut room-size pieces, clean them yourself (see Cleaning instructions. Part II), and roll them up. Advertise them in the local newspaper or go to a swap meet and sell them. If the carpet is in decent shape, it should sell for $3 to $5 a yard if it is a good quality carpet. Otherwise, if it is fairly worn out, you can carpet the garage floor with it. Many people carpet their garage floor to minimize dust and dirt because the carpet attracts the dirt. You can carpet the trunk of your car, the back of your truck, the floors of your car, put room-size pieces in rentals, or give it away to Goodwill or Salvation Army.

You could also give it to your local church or club. Many small churches have Sunday School rooms or recreation rooms that could use the old carpet. Some people use it on backyards and fields to keep the weeds from growing. We have sent used carpet to missionaries in Mexico who really appreciated it. If you live close to the border areas, you might consider that.

If the padding is to be replaced, it is another dirty job. Usually there is no way to reuse the old padding if it has to be replaced. Just throw it out. After the padding is up, the floor will be swept and they are nearly ready to start installing.

You'll notice wood strips with little tacks sticking out of them bordering the edges of your room. These are called "TACKLESS STRIP." They hold the carpet in place and keep a tight grip on it as the carpet is stretched tight to the other side. The installers will check these tack strips to make sure they are nailed down properly and that they are still in good shape. If needed, they will be renailed or replaced. In some cases they will put in a double strip so there will be two of them side by side to ensure a solid, strong fit for the carpeting.

The metal edging is also checked at this time. This is the metal strip where the carpeting meets hard floors or vinyl surfaced floors. It is checked to make sure it can withstand the installation and that it is not broken. If it needs replacing, it will be at that time.

If you know for certain this metal is broken or needs replacing, or you want a different grade of metal for the installation, do not assume that the estimator will take care of it. This is something you should tell the dealer when you BUY the carpeting so the estimator can figure this in when he gives you the total price. Otherwise it may be an add-on charge later.

If the carpet to be installed is a glue-down type of installation, the floor will be inspected for cracks or unevenness. These will be fixed and the floor properly cleaned. It will be swept, mopped and probably mopped again because there cannot be any dirt on the floor when the adhesive goes down.

If new padding is to be installed, it will be at this time. It is laid in place and cut to fit the entire room. The padding will be butted up next to the wood tack strip and the metal. The seams are then taped together. The edges of the entire room are glued or stapled to keep the pad in place while the carpet is being kicked into place. The padding should run crossways from the way the carpet is running (this is the general rule with regular padding). In other words, the seams on the pad will not match up with the seams on the carpet. This is an IMPORTANT thing to watch out for—that the seams do not match when laying the carpet down.

NOW THE CARPET GOES IN. It is cut and loosely fitted in all the rooms. The seams are put in with a hot iron and melting glue tape. This method of seaming carpets has proven to be the quickest and most effective for putting seams in carpeting. If done properly, the seams will last the entire life of the carpet.

After the seams are in, the whole carpet will be kicked in with knee kickers except that larger rooms will be stretched in with a power stretcher. The power stretcher is a long tubular piece of equipment that will extend the entire length of the room. It has claws on one side and a lever on top. It grabs the carpet and pulls it up to the wall. These stretchers are expensive tools and are very important in the installation of carpeting.

Humid areas such as the South will make carpet bubble and warp. Be sure that every room, regardless of size, is power stretched to help prevent this. In dryer areas, the smaller rooms can be kicked in and only the larger ones need to be stretched.

When they are stretched, they should be stretched both length and width. We have seen some carpets that were only stretched one way. Consequently, after cleaning or in humid weather, they began rippling the entire length of the opposite stretch.

As the men are working, please watch from a distance and keep the kids away. They move around a lot and can't have anyone in the way as they run the carpet and padding down. Your assistance in this matter would be greatly appreciated by the installers.

You might like to know something about the installer. Because of his work on his knees and picking up heavy rolls of carpeting, usually working harder than most other labor professions, his average life expectancy in the trade is about 10 years. Most men have to drop out because of knee and back problems which are permanent injuries. The work is physically hard and to do the work properly, he has to have a brain in his head too. These men, if they are good, earn every penny they charge. When you are asked to pay the labor bill, don't try to bargain him down to a lower price. To be competitive, his prices have to be in line with the going rate.

WHAT IS THE AVERAGE CHARGE FOR INSTALLATION? At this writing in the early part of 1980, the average per yard price for unfurnished house installation is $1.65-$2.00 per square yard. The average labor bill for a home of 100 sq. yds. will be around $165.00-$200.00 if you have the entire house carpeted. Stairs and glue-down carpets will usually cost a little more.

FINALLY, THE INSTALLATION IS FINISHED! Now you should inspect the job. If you have any questions, get them answered at this time. If the job meets your expectations, pay them now unless you have made previous arrangements with the dealer.

Move your furniture back and start enjoying your new carpeting. There are some things you will notice about the new carpet. At first there probably will be some shedding. This is normal for most carpeting. After a few months of regular use and vacuuming this will disappear. You may notice an occasional long strand sticking up out of the carpet. There are different names for these. Some people call them sprouts. There's nothing wrong with the carpeting. Just *cut* them off level with the pile. Don't pull it out of the backing. If you pull it out, it leaves an air gap underneath and this can lead to future breakdown of fibers around it.

SCRAPS

You're probably going to have some large scraps left over from the job. Your house was not measured wrong. It's just the way the carpet had to be cut because it comes in 12' widths and your room may be 10' wide. Just accept the fact that scraps will be left over.

We recommend you keep these scraps. There are several reasons for it. They can be used as floor mats and door mats; however, don't use these scraps with the hard rough back as a mat on top of the carpet you just installed. The rubbing will break down the fibers of your new carpet. The only type of throw rugs to put down on top of carpeting are the soft-backed carpeting, the kind that can be easily washed in a machine.

Scraps should also be saved for future repairs. Put them in a box, seal up the box and label it, "CARPET SCRAPS." In the future when a stain or other damage calls for a repair job, you have carpet scraps of the same texture and color to make the necessary repairs.

Large pieces of scraps can be taken to a carpet dealer to be bound on the edges. These can be used on uncarpeted floors for area rugs.

For other uses of carpet scraps, see the sections on "Decorating With Scraps," and "Carpeting the Wall."

DECORATING WITH SCRAPS

Some people in America have used their imaginations for every conceivable thing under the sun. This is true also with carpeting. You may try it as a hobby. Carpet scraps are left over after every job, and with each job there are different types and colors of scraps.

Go to a nearby carpet outlet and ask for the leftover scraps. Often the installers bring them back to the stores to be sent to the dump.

You can take these scraps and make your own carpeting by putting them all together in a collage type pattern. You can make symmetrical designs such as circles, triangles, arrows, and different squares, forming a unique floor design.

Carpeting paintings are becoming very popular. You meticulously cut and design landscapes and seascapes—all from the carpet throw always. They can be framed and hung on the wall or sold as a second income.

If you have the spare time and desire to be creative, perhaps these ideas will inspire you to find other uses for these scraps. I'd like to hear from you if you come up with something unique. Send a photo if you can.

THE NEW HOME CARPET

Many people who purchase a newly constructed home (especially tract homes) are given an option by the developer or contractor to either accept the carpeting that comes standard with the house or pay for *upgrading* the quality of the carpeting before they move in.

It's definitely a temptation to spend just $400 or $500 more for the super plush carpet that you've always wanted in your home, knowing that even the most expensive carpet will only add $7 to $10 more on your monthly payment. Surely you can afford it, so you do it.

Yes, it is nice to have quality carpet in your brand new home. There is one thing to think about before you order it—dirt! Every new construction site (even after structures, streets, etc. are in) has plenty of dirt.

It's in your yards because you don't have grass yet. It's in the air. It's in your house. Even if you're the first on the block to put in landscaping, there is no way the dirt will disappear from your house until all your neighbors have landscaped also and everything is sufficiently grown so as to keep dust and dirt down. If your tract areas are anything like others, it may be as much as a year and a half before the dirt, mud, fertilizers, and just plain new construction dust (plaster) and the like start to disappear. What do you think happens to your expensive upgraded carpet during this time? Ruined? No, not quite, but it has so much junk in it that its life expectancy is cut in half. Have you really saved? Not really.

Take our advice if you're moving into a newly constructed home. Accept the carpet that the contractor is offering you. Then, after the initial couple of years is over, go out and see about upgrading. You'll be a lot happier for it.

COMMERCIAL CARPETING

Carpeting comes in two categories: 1. For commercial purposes, and 2. For the home. Commercial carpeting is generally not suitable for the home because it doesn't have a comfortable appearance and feel that most people like at home. It does not lend itself to a relaxing atmosphere.

If you have a high activity area such as recreation room, playroom, hobby room, or a place where a lot of messes are made, we would recommend a commercial grade of carpeting. Your carpet dealer will have both types available.

Commercial grade does not mean cheaper in price though. It is generally more expensive than residential carpeting, because it is made with better material, and it is made to handle wear.

A great deal of testing has been done on commercial carpets for wear. Just about everything you can think of that would happen in a commercial area—a bank lobby, airport terminal, restaurant, etc.—has been tested on these carpets and out of this testing has developed a carpeting that can endure under these conditions.

BEWARE: There are some salespeople out there that will tell you that a carpet meets commercial standards, when in fact it doesn't. So often I've been asked into an office, to give an explanation why their carpet is looking so worn out. What had happened was the carpet salesperson had sold them a residential carpet and told them it was a commercial.

How can you tell? Its simple, all commercial grade carpets have a list of specifications printed of the sample board, such as construction, pile yam, ply, gauge, stitches, pile height, pile weight, primary and secondary backing materials, and flammability test statistics.

RESILIENT FLOORS

When the term resilient flooring is used, it will mean either smooth-surfaced tile or sheet goods. Resilient means its characteristic of being able to return to its original form after being dented with furniture or everyday use.

The manufacturing is accomplished by placing a sheet of vinyl plastic on top of a secondary backing such as asbestos or fiber-based compound, and bonding the two together. It is cut into the desired shape, either tile squares or in a variety of widths, and rolled up.

HOW DO YOU DETERMINE which type of hard floor to buy? It must be noted that resilient flooring comes in many patterns, colors, and types. You must choose which color and pattern will enhance your home. As far as the type is concerned, you must be aware that some types are better suited for a particular chore than others.

There are on the market resilient floors that have a very soft spongy texture, making it comfortable to stand upon. Some types are so thick that if you were to drop a glass, it probably would not break. These types are excellent for soundproofing especially in upstairs rooms or in an upstairs condominium or apartment. They are also excellent for bathrooms because they are comfortable to stand on, are not slippery, are easily cleaned, and tend to remain at room temperature on the surface.

A MAJOR DISADVANTAGE to these soft floors is that the softer they are, the easier they may be damaged, either by sharp objects or indentations from the legs of stools and chairs. There are furniture leg protectors that are occasionally sold in floor covering stores.

Over all, the best selection for resilient floors in the average home is the harder of the soft goods.

If you decide to buy tile squares and want to keep it clean, by all means STAY AWAY FROM the tile with engraved designs in it. Dirt and wax builds up in these grooves and holes and you may never get it out.

If you are going to install these tile squares in BATHROOMS OR KITCHENS where ODORS build up in these grooves and holes you may put wax on it to seal the seams. If you don't, spills and general bad odors will work down in between the tile squares and then the odor will be PERMANENT.

With the permanently waxed (no-wax) floor tiles, you don't use a wax but a product designed by the manufacturer may be put on the surface to seal it.

Whenever possible, vinyl sheet goods (as opposed to the tile squares above) should be used in kitchens and bathrooms.

THE INSTALLATION of resilient flooring is generally quite expensive, sheet goods being more costly to install than tile. However, if the job is done by a qualified professional and the product is of any decent quality, you may never need to replace it again.

For those who wish to install their own resilient flooring, may we suggest that if you stick to self-stick tile squares and follow the simple directions, just maybe you will be satisfied with the result. For most sheet goods, let the Pro's do it. You'll never forgive yourself if you try to tackle this one without prior experience.

There is now several new resilient floors (sheet goods) that have recently come out. These are easy to install see next page (other types).

COVING

Some people prefer to have their resilient flooring curved up their walls a couple of inches. This is known as COVING and is not only quite attractive but it makes the cleaning and general maintenance of your floor easier. At the same time, this is an EXPENSIVE procedure and should be done only by the most qualified of flooring installers.

MAINTENANCE PROCEDURES

These resilient floors are made to take it. They are sturdy and will look good for years, but from time to time it is necessary to properly clean and, on occasion, get up one of those hard to get spills.

You will be able to prevent a spill from turning into a stain mainly be getting the spill up fast with a damp cloth.

Your main line of defense is to maintain a good protective coat of wax on the average floor. For the no-wax floors, treat them regularly with the manufacturer's recommended products and, if you don't know what to use, call your local floor covering distributor.

Each flooring will have its own directions for you to follow. But what about those floors that you don't know anything about and were there before you moved in? General directions are:

No-Wax Floor

1. Wash with mild detergent using sponge mop.

2. Use manufacturer products as recommended on label.

3. Although waxing & stripping are not needed, you must keep it clean and use chemical treatments periodically.

Regular Floor

1. Wash with strong detergent using sponge mop or bristle brush.

2. On occasion, use fine steel wool and powdered detergent to get old wax up.

3. Wax floors as needed but don't allow more than 3 coats of wax to build-up.

The above procedures are standard for the two types of floors. The below mentioned problems will be true to both.

HEEL MARKS are usually the most common problem. Use a damp rag with either a household spray cleaner or use some liquid wax in the rag and rub it up. If this fails, use the finest grade of steel wool in the lumber or hardware store (0000 gauge), the rub the heel mark with liquid wax very lightly. Wash and re-wax your floor.

Paint can usually come up easily if gotten to quickly. Should there be a delay you may need to use steel wool as with heel marks.

GUM or TAR need only be scraped up with a spoon. It's easiest when the gum or tar have hardened. This can be speeded up by rubbing them with an ice cube. Once hard, just use steel wool and wax as above.

MUSTARD, COFFEE, TEA, FRUIT JUICE STAIN—after wiping up, use steel wool and wax as above but you might take hydrogen peroxide in a dampened paper towel folder over and laid over the stain. Step on it for a couple of minutes, then clean and wax the floor.

OTHER TYPES (NOT AS COMMON)

There are other types of resilient floors that may be encountered such as cork, asphalt tile, linoleum, leather, rubber, plus a newer type of sheet goods (flexible-elastic) which comes under different names but is glued or stapled down around the edges & seams only. It can be wrinkled up and bent but it always returns to its original shape. It is very durable and it is especially useful on floors that may move, either with expansion or contraction.

Armstrong (tm) has recently come out with a do-it-yourself kit for these newer flexible vinyl floors. It is easy to use and if directions are followed exactly, it will result in a beautiful job.

HARDWOOD (PARQUET)

In years gone by hardwood floors were by far the most popular floors. As asbestos tile and carpeting came into predominance and the cost of good hardwood floors became more expensive, they slowly faded from widespread use.

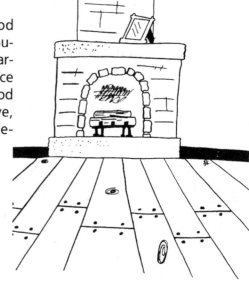

Those old wood floors had some irritating problems. Probably the main one was that they all looked alike. Everybody that had a hardwood floor had one just like his neighbor. Today people like variety and want to be different. They like for their homes to be an expression of them and what they think is nice. So with that kind of thinking surfacing, of course, the same floor as the Jones just has to go.

Another main problem was maintenance. Getting dirt up was easy—just dust mop and shake it out the back door, making sure the wind is blowing away from you so it all doesn't fly back inside. Do you remember those days?

But the other half of the maintenance was ROUGH—WAXING and POLISHING. Even sand paper wouldn't get out deep scratches. Every conscientious housewife had to be some sort of an expert in wood repair and refinishing. How about those who varnished their floors? Boy, what a job that was. Try doing that with the windows closed.

Well, today thank goodness most all of those problems have been resolved. The people who made those early floors were smart enough to realize that their product had better take on a new look or else they would be out of business. They came up with wood tiles called PARQUET. Different hardwoods (Teak to Oak and all those in between) were arranged in beautiful patterns. They oiled and waxed them and invented new permanent ways to install them. They come not only in squares, but in long planks or smaller pieces which are fit together to form patterns. With some manufacturers, the designs are unlimited.

The over-all picture today of the wood parquet floor is innovative— beautiful in all respects—warm and comfortable—easy to clean and maintain—and repairs can be done by the homeowner with ease. The major maintenance cost is more expensive than ceramic but the chances of ever having to replace a part of your floor is practically non-existent. (Do keep a couple of extra pieces just in case.)

The cost of materials and installation is high and we DO NOT REC-OMMEND wood for KITCHENS OR BATHROOMS, OR any room where there is a moisture problem.

In purchasing parquet flooring, be very careful about where you buy it and WHO MAKES it. A good floor will cost some money, so if you have decided to buy wood, expect to pay anywhere from $4 per sq. ft. and up. That price includes installation. Here again, your parquets are specialty floors. and should only be installed by skilled professionals.

By all means be careful of bargains in wood floors. We have actually seen some advertised at $.99 per square foot. Upon examination one can see how they do it. They use cheap, poor quality wood. It is about half the thickness of quality wood. The finish used is only superficial. The waxes, if any, are only surface waxes, not the good baked-in waxes that are available with the quality goods. These cheaper floors will crack and split after a short time, and whatever finish is there starts to wear off fast.

CERAMIC TILE

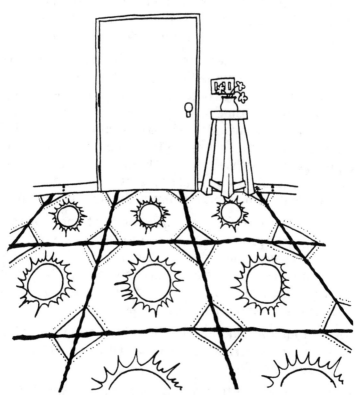

Ceramic tile is made of clay and other organic materials, and then baked in an oven at high temperatures. The finished product is hardened enough to be very suitable for placement into nearly all flooring areas (if desired), and will last, for all practical purposes, forever.

A point that should be considered about using ceramic tile on floors in BATHROOMS AND KITCHENS. Again, you have the problem of spilled substances with undesirable odors. The surface of most ceramic tile is glazed, making it non-porous so that moisture cannot seep through it. However, the areas in between each tile are filled with a substance called GROUT. This is POROUS and WILL ABSORB moisture and undesirable odors.

For KITCHENS and BATHROOMS, we highly RECOMMEND that you NOT use porous (unglazed) ceramic tile. Over the years, you will regret it. There are sealers that may be used, but by having to periodically treat your floors with these sealers, you are doing away with the main purpose of a ceramic floor—no maintenance.

Another factor to keep in mind is that ceramic tile floors are more SLIPPERY when wet than other types of floors.

The installation cost is quite EXPENSIVE and so is the product itself. Ceramic floors are a specialty floor and should only be installed by highly experienced professionals. In many cases, your subflooring will have to be reinforced underneath the house to hold the weight of the tiles.

Should you install ceramic tile flooring in any part of your house, be sure to buy at least 5 extra tiles to save with your important belongings. Tile patterns change constantly. If a section of your tile floor should crack or break, you would need the extra tiles to replace the broken ones. For all practical purposes though, if a ceramic tile floor is installed properly, the only thing that could hurt it is if something heavy was dropped on it. Or a good earthquake!

OTHER TYPES

Other types of floors would include SLATE, MARBLE, FLAT STONES AND BRICK. Some very attractive floors have been designed from bricks. These are of hard floors not usually found in floor covering stores but more often through a masonry outlet.

ORIENTAL RUGS

(MORROCAN - PERSIAN - CHINESE -HAND-MADE - MACHINE MADE)

Oriental rugs and their origins have been discussed in some detail in the Introduction and History part of this manual. At this point, I would like to make possible suggestions on the use and cleaning of your Oriental rug.

Rugs are best used to either frame in a piece of furniture or to frame in a room. If you have a beautiful piece of furniture and you wish people to take notice of it, place an Oriental carpet underneath it. It will certainly command the attention you are looking for. Then, naturally, the attention will pass down to the rug itself.

If the rug is large and exceptional in quality or design, center your entire room around it. Let IT become the main center of attraction. Be sure that you don't have any parties while the rug is down. One of the nicest things about these rugs is you can just roll them up and move them aside if it looks as though activities will harm them.

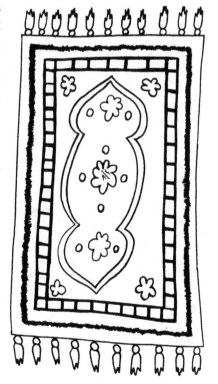

One of the most beautiful settings for Oriental rugs is either on ceramic tile floors or, better, yet, on wood parquet floors. On either one, the Oriental rug will get its maximum glory. The floor seems to set off the rug and the rug sets off the floor.

As always, there are some factors to consider. The COST is HIGH for any hand-made quality rug. Some have paid as high as $250,000 for just an antique area rug. On the other hand, you can find decent, small hand-made rugs for around $100. So your cost range on these is wide and the opportunity to make a deal is very good. The markup ranges from 50% to 100% so you have room to dicker.

MACHINE-MADE ORIENTALS: These, too, are quite beautiful and made out of just as fine materials—usually high-grade wools. However, they do not have any real value. It is only the handmade rugs that will draw an appreciable value. The machine-made rugs are just reproductions of the valuable man-made ones.

CLEANING

For general cleaning of the hand-made or machine-made Oriental rug, you should vacuum at least once a week SLOWLY. Be careful not to get the rug end fringes caught into the rotating brushes. Put your vacuum on its lowest setting so as to insure the best contact with the Oriental.

For wet cleaning on small rugs, do it yourself. You'll get wet but you will save a lot of money. Fill your bathtub with lukewarm water to the half-way level. Add a mild detergent that was made for wool only. Loosely roll up the rug and place it in the tub. Let it soak for about ½ hour. After the detergent has had time to saturate in, then start unrolling it under the water. With a very soft bristle brush, scrub the pile lightly. When you have finished, change the water and rinse the carpet in it thoroughly using cool or cold water. You may have to rinse more than once.

Now, roll it up tight, squeezing out most of the water and take it outside to dry in the sunlight. With good sunlight, it should be ready to turn over in about 2 hours. Let the back-side get dry to the touch (about 1 hour), then turn it back over for an additional hour and it's done. The whole process of actually cleaning can be accomplished in about one hour once you've done it a couple of times.

But what about those white fringes on the ends? Every third or fourth cleaning will require that you bleach those fringes. Whatever you do, don't put the bleach in the wash water. Bleaching is a completely separate action that is done after your rug has been washed and dried.

To bleach the fringes: Measure the length of the fringe. Then fill the tub with hot water to that depth. If the fringe is 3", then you only want 3" of water in the tub. Next, lay an edge of the rug over the side of the tub so that only the fringes are in the water. You might want to weight the rug down to ensure that it doesn't move by mistake. Add some powdered bleach (at least a full cup) to the water and stir it around. Then let the fringes sit in it for an hour and rinse it out. Do the same to the other end. You've just saved yourself as much as $65 for the cleaning of a small rug.

Larger rugs should be cleaned by a professional rug cleaner. For your own peace of mind, try to deal with those who advertise that they clean Oriental rugs. It isn't that these rugs can be ruined so easily—actually the opposite is true. They are very sturdy and can take an awful lot of abuse. However, the carpet cleaners today are inexperienced with multiple color wool fabrics. So, rather than having the unlearned do it and possibly ruin it, you should stay with the one who is familiar with the peculiarities of the Orientals.

RENTAL PROPERTY

Many people have rental property today and most who have them wish that they didn't. In working with rental income property for 14 years, these are some of the recurring problems we have encountered.

About a third of the renters don't care about your property and will not take care of it. Consequently, the carpets and floors are destroyed in a very short time. If no pets are allowed, you can be sure that they will have a couple of cats, a dog, a couple of birds, and maybe a pet rabbit or hamster. Because the pets aren't allowed to go out, and are not allowed in the complex in the first place, they do their business on the floor, trying, of course, to hit the newspaper so nicely laid down for them.

If it is a family complex where children are allowed, wet diapers are left on the carpet, gum and candy are found stuck in the carpet, and if anything can be spilled on the carpet, it will be.

Adults do exactly the same thing. They raise snakes. They overhaul their motorcycles in the living room. The do-it-your-selfers saw and paint their creations on the carpet. The man of the house installs a stereo system by running the speaker cords under the carpet, ripping it up where needed. The couches and chairs always seem to have broken legs which rip and snag the carpet as they are pulled across the room. The lady of the house wants house plants so she puts unprotected potted plants on the carpet and then over waters the plants. After several weeks, the plants die and she throws them out; but, behold, she still has house plants growing out of the faded brown spot on the carpet—mushrooms! The daughter decides to iron a dress and the kitchen table is still filled with last night's dirty dishes, so she irons on the carpet, laying the hot iron on the floor. When finished and much to her amazement, there is a nice crispy melted iron spot in the carpet and she explains, "We'll, I didn't know."

Many renters don't vacuum because its' too much trouble to borrow from the manager or neighbors. The waterbed is a must so it goes in without liners or guarantees. Then it bursts open when the cat digs her claws into it and leaves a swimming pool on the floor. Parties are always a must—spilling drinks, dips, and occasionally barbecue pits over on the floor. Ashtrays seem hard to get these days as the cigarette ashes and butts end up on the floor. The toilet overflows and the only one who hears about it are the tenants below who have water dripping from the ceiling onto their carpet.

After a life like this, who could be sane? Not even the guy responsible, so he quietly gets high on drugs or booze, goes to the bedroom, sits down on the bed, slashed his wrist with a razor, leaving a mess on the carpet.

Who has to pay for all this? Why, you do! We don't mean to sound negative but the above is an accumulation of just *some* of the many experiences we have run into in the rental housing field. We could make many suggestions on how to alleviate most of these problems and how to screen out potential undesirable tenants, but to do this would be against recent government rulings. The landlord basically has no rights and cannot govern his own property. So we will stick strictly to recommendations for floor coverings for the rental property. The above incidences are just to let you know what to expect if you decide to become a landlord.

There are two categories to be considered when buying floor covering for rental units:

FAMILY AND YOUNG ADULT: It is best not to spend much money on floor covering here. Life expectancy of even fine quality goods is 5—7 years. With a proper maintenance program you should expect maximum life from even the low grade floor coverings. Use low priced pad (1/2" 4 lb. rebound or 1/2" 1.5 lb. prime urethane). If it gets wet it won't be lost, and in the event of early carpet replacement, the pad can be saved, (except from urine damage).

The carpet you choose should be 100% Nylon, with a low pile. Either a short closed loop or a short Frieze. Possible even and inexpensive shag. The colors most suitable are the natural tones (browns, avocado green, dark rust).

Hard floors should be non grooved or non engraved tile, or inexpensive sheet goods. With the hard floors in kitchen, dining room, outside door entry ways and bathrooms.

All outside porches, landing or steps leading to apartments should have artificial turf glued down in front of the doors.

SENIOR CITIZEN APARTMENTS: The older folks are for the most part your best renters. They don't move around as often and can usually be expected to stay in an apartment for years. They also take good care of their place, so if you can afford it, upgrading the floor covering will add comfort to their lives and increase the value of your property. Use turf and hard floors in the same way as the other units.

A NOTE OF CAUTION: For the protection of all the carpets in your rentals. Don't allow the tenant to clean their own carpets. Have only a professional do it.

The average life of a rental unit's carpeting is 5 years with a well-programmed maintenance program. We have had them last up to 10 years, but on the other hand we've gone in and replaced them 30 days after they were installed. The reason for 30-day replacement was because of damage done by the tenants, not because the carpet or the installation weren't any good.

When you buy carpeting for your rental units, the more you buy now, the less you will pay later as the price goes up every 90 to 120 days as of this writing. You should keep enough extra carpet and pad on hand to redo 1 out of every 10 units. Purchase plenty of extra padding, you will save a tremendous amount of money in the time ahead on repairs and replacement.

In the kitchens and bathrooms, use the least expensive vinyl asbestos tile or vinyl sheet goods. It's surprising how quickly they, too, can be destroyed.

If you are the landlord of more than a few units, it is a very good idea to have at least 2 well-maintained vacuum cleaners made available to your tenants. It may also be beneficial for you to even sell vacuum cleaners on a time payment basis to your tenants. Many renters can't afford to buy one outright but may well be able to afford maybe $10 per month added on to their rent. If they use it, it will save you money in the long run.

MOTEL CARPET MAINTENANCE

This section will be brief but is included for those of you who happen to have a motel and all the problems that go with them. The carpets in motels that I have been in and have stayed in range from the best to the worst. In my estimation, 80% of the motels use the wrong kind of carpeting and don't properly maintain what they do have.

Carpeting for motels should be COMMERCIAL GRADE with short, dense tightly woven pile. The pad should be heavy-duty (7 lb. Rebound or 3 lb. Prime Urethane).

Carpeting should be vacuumed thoroughly in all traffic areas after every 7 to 10 uses. Light vacuuming can be done after every 2 to 3 uses.

If the location of your motel is on the beach or desert or in an area of blowing dust. Daily vacuuming may very well be necessary.

Have the maids keep the manager informed as to the condition of carpeting in each room. If a spill or stain is found, don't have anyone except a person with whom you have the fullest of confidence come in to try to remove the stains. So often a maid unknowingly will put the wrong cleaning agent on the spot which sets the stain so that it may never come out.

If possible, use vinyl for all entry ways into every room and good, absorbent doormats. On outside entrances and sidewalks, the artificial turf is excellent. The greatest damage is done to the ground-level rooms where tar and oil is tracked in from the parking lot.

A good maintenance program for a busy motel will include the proper carpet cleaning of each room after 60 to 70 uses.

NOTE: If commercial carpeting is out of the question because of the cost factor, other durable carpets made for the home will do the job fairly well. Do not use shags, plushes or cut loops. Frieze or level or multiple level loops are all OK.

CARPET BUYERS DIRECTIVE

BEFORE LEAVING THE HOUSE TO PURCHASE CARPET, FOLLOW THESE STEPS:

1) KNOW HOW MUCH MONEY YOU CAN AFFORD TO SPEND. TRY ALWAYS TO DEAL IN CASH FOR ADDED BARGAIN POWER. (PAGE 32)

2) KNOW APPROX. HOW MUCH CARPET YOU WILL NEED. TO GET AN APPROXIMATE SQUARE YARD FIGURE: DIVIDE TOTAL SQUARE FOOTAGE OF FLOOR AREA TO BE COVERED BY 9. A.) IF TOTAL SO. YD. FIGURE IS 110 OR BELOW, ADD 6% B.) IF TOTAL SO. YD. FIGURE IS 111-150, ADD 5% C.) IF TOTAL SO. YD. FIGURE IS ABOVE 150 ADD 4%. NOTE: THIS METHOD OF CALCULATION IS NOT EXACT BUT WILL GIVE YOU A CLOSE ENOUGH ESTIMATE TO PROTECT YOU FROM THE DISHONEST OR INCOMPETENT CARPET ESTIMATOR. IT ALSO WILL SERVE YOU IN YOUR OWN PRICING ESTIMATES. (PAGE 42)

3) KNOW WHAT COLORS WILL GO WITH YOUR FURNISHINGS, DRAPERIES, LIGHTING AND SOIL AROUND YOUR HOME. (PAGE 33-36)

4) KNOW WHAT TYPE OF CARPET WILL MEET YOUR NEEDS. (PAGE 23-26)

5) IF POSSIBLE, KNOW WHETHER OR NOT YOU WILL NEED PADDING. (PAGE 61)

6) ALLOW AT LEAST A FULL DAY TO SHOP AROUND AT SEVERAL STORES. (PAGE 52)

7) DETERMINE AHEAD OF TIME WHO YOU ARE GOING TO SEE AND IF POSSIBLE, THE REPUTATION OF THOSE DEALERS. (PAGE 63)

8) BE CERTAIN TO TAKE A NOTE PAD AND PEN. (PAGE 53)

ONCE INSIDE EACH STORE LOOK FOR THESE ITEMS

1) TYPE OF CARPET FIBER WITH NYLON BEING PREFERRED OVER ALL (PAGE 23-26)

2) TYPE OF CARPET BACKING WITH THE SYNTHETIC PREFERRED (PAGE 26-27)

3) IF CARPET MEETS OR EXCEEDS THE FHA STANDARDS IT WILL STATE SO ON THE BACK OF THE CARPET SAMPLE.

4) IF THE CARPET HAS A GUARANTEE IT WILL STATE SO ON THE BACK OF THE CARPET SAMPLE. READ THE SMALL PRINT AND MAKE A NOTE OF IT. (PAGE 54)

5) IF CARPET HAS ANTI-STATIC CONTROL IT WILL STATE SO ON BACK OF CARPET SAMPLE. (PAGE 28)

6) IF CARPET HAS SOIL RETARDANT IN IT, IT WILL SO STATE ON THE BACK OF CARPET SAMPLE. (PAGE 62)

ALL OF THE ABOVE ITEMS ARE SOMETIME DECLARED BY CARPET DEALERS, BUT UNLESS THEY ARE STATED BY THE MANUFACTURERS BY IRONED ON PATCHES ON THE BACKS OF CARPET SAMPLES IT WOULD BE BEST NOT TO COUNT ON THESE CLAIMS TO BE TRUE, UNLESS OF COURSE IT IS PRINTED ON THE SAMPLE BOOK ITSELF.

7) ASK ABOUT INSTALLATION GUARANTEES; IT IS ONE YEAR BY LAW IN MOST STATES. IF MENTIONED TO BE LONGER THAN THIS, BE SURE TO ASK FOR IT IN WRITING.

8) IF PADDING IS NEEDED: COMPARE PADDING FOR FIRMNESS/THICK-NESS/PRICE/COMFORT. ONCE IT IS DETERMINED WHICH STORE YOU ARE GOING TO DO BUSINESS WITH, ASK FOR A SMALL (3 SO. INCH) PIECE OF PADDING AND KEEP IT UNTIL THE DAY OF INSTALLATION. WHEN THE PAD IS INSTALLED COMPARE IT WITH THE PIECE YOU HAVE. IT IS NOT AN UNCOMMON PRACTICE FOR A DEALER TO SELL A CUSTOMER ONE GRADE OF PAD AND THEN INSTALL A LESSER QUALITY. (PAGE 59-61)

9) GET ITEMIZED FIRM PRICES FROM THE DEALER IN WRITING ON CARPET, PAD AND INSTALLATION. NOTE: PRICES ARE GOING UP ALL THE TIME, SO BE SURE TO ASK THE DEALER HOW LONG THAT PRICE IS GOOD FOR.

10) AS YOU COMPARE PRICES FROM STORE TO STORE, MAKE CERTAIN TO ONLY COMPARE STYLES WITH STYLES. DON'T COMPARE SHAGS IN ONE STORE AND PLUSHES IN ANOTHER, THEN BUY THE SHAG BECAUSE ITS CHEAPER.

11) AS YOU MAKE NOTES TO YOURSELF, CHECK YARN LENGTH, DEN-SITY, FIBER, AND TWISTS PER INCH. NOTE: IF CARPET WEIGHTS ARE USED THEY ARE AN EXCELLENT WAY OF COMPARISON EXCEPT NOT ALL CARPET MANUFACTURERS ARE DILIGENT IN SUPPLYING THEIR DEALERS WITH THIS INFORMATION, SO IF YOU SHOULD ASK A DEALER WHAT A PARTICULAR PILE WEIGHT MAY BE, HE PROBABLY WONT KNOW. BUT YOU CAN ALWAYS COMPARE THE ABOVE 4 CHARACTERISTICS WITHOUT THE AID OF THE DEALER. (PAGES 20, 23 & 43)

12) GET A FIRM COMMITMENT FROM THE DEALER WHEN IT CAN BE INSTALLED AND THEN, FOR YOUR OWN PEACE OF MIND, ALLOW 2 WEEKS MORE (PAGE 68)

13) ASK IF THE PARTICULAR PIECE OF CARPET THAT YOU ARE LOOKING AT HAS ANY ADDITIONAL INFORMATION SUCH AS BROCHURES OR FLYERS FROM THE MANUFACTURER.

14) AFTER SEVERAL STORES HAVE BEEN VISITED GO AND RELAX WHILE YOU DISCUSS THE PROS AND CONS OF WHAT YOU'VE FOUND. (PAGE 55)

15) IF NEEDED, GO BACK A SECOND TIME. ONCE YOU'VE DETERMINED WHO YOU WILL DEAL WITH YOU SHOULD NOW ATTEMPT TO GET A BETTER PRICE, UNLESS YOU FEEL THAT YOU ARE ALREADY GET-TING THE BEST DEAL ALWAYS REMEMBER, THE DEALER HAS TO MAKE A PROFIT IN ORDER TO STAY IN BUSINESS. (PAGE 53)

THESE ITEMS YOU SHOULD LOOK OUT FOR:

"BEWARE OF STRANGE SALESMAN BEARING FREE GIFTS." ALSO ADS

1) "FREE PAD WITH WHOLE HOUSE CARPETED." DON'T BELIEVE IT. THIS IS USUALLY THE BAIT AND SWITCH GAME. THE PAD THEY SAY IS FREE IS OF THE POOREST QUALITY, AND WHEN YOU WANT TO UPGRADE YOU PAY AS MUCH AS ANYONE ELSE. IN ANY CASE THE PAD IS NOT FREE EVEN IF YOU ACCEPT THE POOR QUALITY BRAND, THE PRICE IS STILL FIGURED INTO THE PRICE OF THE CARPET. (PAGE 50)

NOTE: SOMETIMES IT IS POSSIBLE TO GET FREE PAD WHEN PURCHAS-ING REMNANTS BUT ONLY IF THE DEALER IS GETTING A DECENT PRICE FOR THAT REMNANT.

2) "FREE INSTALLATION WHEN WHOLE HOUSE IS CARPETED." AGAIN NOTHING IS FREE, AND NEVER IS THE INSTALLATION FREE. (PAGE 50)

3) LOOK OUT FOR SPECIAL SALES, THAT OFFER 50 to 70% OFF THE REGU-LAR SALE PRICE. IF THEY CAN KNOCK MORE THAN HALF THE PRICE OFF AND STILL MAKE A PROFIT THEY ARE CHARGING TOO MUCH AND CAN'T BE TRUSTED ANY WAY. IT'S VERY LIKELY THAT YOU WILL BE ABLE TO FIND A DEALER WHOSE REGULAR PRICES ARE THE SAME OR EVEN LOWER THAN THE ADVERTISERS SPECIALS. (PAGE 51)

4) "100%" FINANCING: IF A DEALER OFFERS FINANCING THRU HIS OWN FIRM OR CREDIT CARDS, THERE WILL BE A PRETTY GOOD CHANCE HIS PRICES ARE HIGHER THAN THE DEALER WHO OFFERS NO FINANCING. THIS WOULD NOT NECESSARILY HE TRUE IF THE DEALER WAS OFFERING FINANCING FROM AN OUTSIDE LENDING INSTITUTION THAT WOULD BUY THE CONTRACT FROM THE DEALER.

5) "CARPET THE WHOLE HOUSE (1000) SQ FT. FOR $579. 00." THESE ADS OF COURSE, WILL VARY WITH PRICE AND AREA TO BE COVERED. THEY ARE USED TO GET YOU INTO THE STORE. ONCE YOU SEE THE QUALITY OF CARPET THAT THE AD IS DESCRIBING, YOU WILL CER-TAINLY WANT TO BUY A BETTER GRADE OF CARPET. SOMETIMES THESE LOW PRICES WILL INCLUDE PADDING ALSO BUT RARELY WILL THE TAX BE INCLUDED. THE ONLY TIME A PERSON MAY REALLY TAKE ADVANTAGE OF THIS TYPE OF SPECIAL IS FOR USE IN A RENTAL

UNIT. TO FIND OUT THE ACTUAL PRICE PER YARD OF THE CARPET IN THE ABOVE EXAMPLE, TAKE THE 1000 SO. YDS AND DIVIDE BY 9. THIS EQUALS 111 SO. YDS. NOW MULTIPLY 111 SQ. YDS. BY $1. 65 TO DETERMINE THE APPROX COST OF THE INSTALLATION. THIS AMOUNTS TO $183. 15. SUBTRACT THAT AMOUNT FROM THE SALE PRICE OF $579. 00 WHICH TOTALS $395. 85 THEN DIVIDE THAT BY YOUR ALLOWED YARDAGE OF 111. THIS WILL GIVE THE PER YARD PRICE OF $3. 57. ADS ARE THERE TO ATTRACT YOUR ATTENTION, $0 READ THEM CAREFULLY.

6) "THREE DAYS ONLY", "SPECIAL TRAIN LOAD SALE," ETC. THESE SPECIALS ARE USUALLY HELD BY THE SAME STORES 20 TIMES A YEAR. SO DON'T BE INTIMIDATED AND HURRY OUT TO SPEND YOUR MONEY...ON THIS CHANCE OF A LIFETIME SALE. THE ONLY SALE THAT MIGHT, AND I SAY MIGHT, REALLY SAVE YOU MONEY IS THE GOING OUT OF BUSINESS SALE. BUT TOO OFTEN THESE SALES DON'T REALLY OFFER THE GREAT SAVINGS THAT PEOPLE BELIEVE THEY ARE GETTING. ALWAYS SHOP AROUND AND KNOW THE PRICES OF THE PRODUCTS YOU NEED.

7) NOTE OF CAUTION: WHEN PURCHASING THICK PLUSH CARPETS. IF THERE ARE GOING TO BE ELDERLY PEOPLE WHO HAVE A HARD TIME WALKING, YOU MIGHT CONSIDER AVOIDING THESE THICKER CARPETS. YOU WILL FIND YOURSELF GETTING TIRED AS YOU WALK BACK AND FORTH DURING THE DAY, BUT IT BECOMES A REAL OBSTACLE COURSE FOR THE AGED OR HANDICAPPED.

8) NOTE OF CAUTION: WHEN CARPET IS NICE TO FEEL, IT TENDS TO GET DIRTY FASTER THAN THE STIFFER CARPET. IT SHOULD NOT BE IN- STALLED ANYWHERE NEAR A KITCHEN, WHERE CHILDREN OR PETS ARE, OR WHERE SMOKERS LIVE. YOU SHOULD NEVER PURCHASE A SOFT CARPET THAT IS SCULPTURED; FOR THE SOFT YARN SOON FALLS INTO THE SCULPTURED AREAS AND THE DESIGN BECOMES OBSCURE. UNDER NO CIRCUMSTANCES SHOULD YOU GO BARE- FOOT ON THIS CARPET, IT STAINS VERY FAST.

9) WHEN AN ESTIMATOR COMES OUT TO YOUR HOUSE TO MEASURE, BE CERTAIN OF THE APPROX AMOUNT OF CARPET YOU NEED. SO FEW PEOPLE ACTUALLY KNOW HOW TO MEASURE YARDAGE THAT IT OFFERS AN OPPORTUNITY TO THE UNSCRUPULOUS DEALER TO DRASTICALLY OVER MEASURE AND POCKET THE DIFFERENCE. (PAGE 42-45... MEASUREMENTS AND REMNANTS)

10) WHEN THE INSTALLERS COME OUT TO PUT THE CARPET IN, IF PADDING IS NEEDED, CHECK YOUR PIECE OF PAD WITH THAT THAT IS BEING INSTALLED. IT IS NOT UNUSUAL FOR A DEALER TO SWITCH PADS. USUALLY THE INSTALLER DOES NOT KNOW ABOUT THIS CHANGE.

11) WHEN PAYING FOR THE CARPET DON'T PAY FOR THE LABOR IN ADVANCE. (PAGE 64 ACTUAL PURCHASE OF THE CARPET)

12) DON'T UP-GRADE THE CARPET IN A NEW HOME. (PAGE 71)

13) IF THE SALESMAN IS SELLING YOU COMMERCIAL CARPET HAVE IT VERIFIED BY THE STATISTICS PRINTED ON THE SAMPLE BACK. (PAGE 72)

14) AFTER THE CARPET IS INSTALLED, SAVE ALL LARGE SCRAPS. (PAGE 69)

15) IF RESILIENT FLOORS HAVE BEEN INSTALLED, SAVE ALL SCRAPS THAT ARE LARGER THAN ONE SO. FT. BOTH FOR POSSIBLE REPAIRS, OR IN THE EVENT OF A LARGE LEFT-OVER, IT MAY BE USED FOR COUNTER TOPS, DRAWER LININGS, SHELF COVERS, OR EVEN ON WALLS THAT GET DIRT, SUCH AS BEHIND THE STOVE.

16) IF WOOD PARQUET HAS BEEN INSTALLED. SAVE ALL LEFT OVER PIECES FOR POSSIBLE REPAIRS. IF THERE ARE QUITE A FEW PIECES LEFT OVER YOU MIGHT MAKE HOT PAN PLATES, OR NEW TABLE TOPS, OR EVEN BOOK ENDS

NOTE: WITH THE MANY BEAUTIFUL DESIGNS IN WOOD PARQUAY AND PLANK FLOORING, YOU MAY EVEN DECORATE AN ENTIRE WALL WITH IT.

17) IF CERAMIC TILES HAVE BEEN INSTALLED. SAVE THE EXTRA TILES FOR POSSIBLE REPAIRS, OR HOT PAN HATES, TABLE TOPS, EVEN FIRE PLACE HEARTHS.

NOTE OF CAUTION: FOR THE DO-IT-YOURSELFER. IF YOU ARE INSTALL-ING YOUR OWN CERAMIC TILE, BE CERTAIN TO MEASURE THEM AT THE TIME OF PURCHASE. MANY FOREIGN TILES ARE MADE TO METRIC MEASUREMENTS AND AT THE TIME OF EXPORT, THEN CONVERTED OVER TO INCHES. THESE MEASUREMENTS ARE RARELY ACCURATE AND USUALLY FALL SHORT, SOME AS SHORT AS 1/4 INCH THIS COULD CAUSE QUITE A SHORTAGE OVER A LARGE AREA.

18) NOTE OF CAUTION: ON BUYING (HANDMADE) ORIENTAL, INVEST-MENT QUALITY CARPETS THE SERIOUS BUYER IS MAKING AN IMPORTANT INVESTMENT* SO DON'T BUY ON IMPULSE. FIRST EDUCATE YOURSELF BY READING BOOKS, WHICH ARE AVAILABLE AT MOST BOOKSTORES; TALK TO THE PEOPLE WHO ARE IN THE TRADE, GET THEIR OPINIONS AND IF POSSIBLE GET THE CARPET TO TRY IT OUT IN YOUR HOME FOR A COUPLE OF DAYS. BUYING AN ORIENTAL IS SIMILAR TO BUYING W/W CARPET IN THAT YOU SHOULD CONSIDER LIGHTING, FURNISHINGS, DRAPERIES AND LO-CATION. PLUS WITH THE ORIENTAL YOU MUST ALSO CONSIDER INVESTMENT POTENTIAL. ONCE YOU'VE CHOSEN THE CARPET YOU WANT, HAVE IT APPRAISED BY A PROFESSIONAL. THERE ARE NOT MANY REAL EXPERTS IN THIS FIELD SO BE CAREFUL WATCH OUT FOR ANTIQUE DEALERS WHO PASS THEMSELVES OFF AS BEING CARPET APPRAISERS. USUALLY THEY DON'T KNOW MUCH MORE THAN YOU, WHEN A REAL EXPERT IS CONTACTED, GET THE AP-PRAISAL IN WRITING. TAKE SEVERAL PHOTOGRAPHS (IN COLOR), THEN ENLARGE THEM TO 10 X 8 1/2. PLACE THE APPRAISAL AND PHOTOS IN WITH YOUR VALUABLE PAPERS. THEN YOU SHOULD ALSO INSURE EITHER THE CARPET OR INCREASE THE COVERAGE OF YOUR FURNISHINGS. EMPHASIS ON THEFT, FIRE, FLOOD. FOR THE BEST BUYS IN INVESTMENT GRADE RUGS, STAY WITH IRANIAN, TURKISH AND CAUCASIAN, ESPECIALLY THOSE WITH MIXTURES OF PILE MATERIAL, WOOL AND SILK. BE CERTAIN TO HAVE PAD-DING UNDER YOUR RUG AND BE SURE TO ROTATE THE RUG EVERY SEVERAL MONTHS. IN CASE REPAIRS ARE NEEDED, CONSULT ONLY AN AUTHORIZED ORIENTAL CARPET REPAIRMAN. NEVER ALLOW A MACHINE TO MAKE THE REPAIRS TO YOUR CARPET. FOR MORE DETAILED INFORMATION YOU MIGHT GET THESE BOOKS: RUGS TO RICHES BY CAROLINE BOSLY, ORIENTAL PRIMER BY ARAM JER-REHIAN, RUGS AS AN INVESTMENT BY PARUIZ NEMATI.

PART III
Maintenance

MAINTAINING YOUR CARPETS

Preventative maintenance of a carpet is very similar to going to a dentist. The dentist will tell us all the things we should do to maintain clean white, healthy teeth and gums. He advises us on flossing, brushing after every meal, brushing properly, massaging the gums, eating the right foods, etc. The bottom line is, "WHO HAS THAT KIND OF TIME TO TAKE CARE OF THEIR TEETH?" Some people do but most people don't. They pay to get all that good advice and then don't use it.

I hope that you won't be that way with this manual. The information contained and the instructions given are important in the maintenance of your carpet. It does take a lot of work but so does everything that amounts to anything. If you have anything of value whatsoever, you can be sure that it has to be taken care of and maintained properly to maintain its value.

Carpets which are properly maintained can last 15 to 20 years and longer. This can be expected and you should expect nothing less. If you should ever live in a house longer than that, the carpet may last just as long; but for all practical purposes, properly maintained carpeting in the high-medium to high price range will last 15 to 20 years. For a medium price range you can expect 10 to 15 years of good carpet life. In the low range you can get 10 years at a maximum. In the contract area you might expect 5 to 7 years depending upon the care.

Now that we know how long it's going to last, let's get into MAKING it last that long. You've purchased the carpet and pad, and there's a possibility now that you may be able to purchase some additional items. We

RECOMMEND HIGHLY that you use the ARTIFICIAL TURF for all outside porches—covering the top of the porch and the steps leading up to it, both front and back doors. We also RECOMMEND this in doorways from the garage into carpeted areas. This turf can be purchased at a carpet dealership. It is very inexpensive and with a few simple instructions, you can install it yourself as long as you are not covering a large area.

If all you're attempting to do is cover the porch areas, buy an all-purpose, all-weather glue (1 or 2 quarts). Get a slotted trowel with a 3/32" notch in it. Any hardware store or lumber yard will have this. This is for spreading the adhesive. Clean the entire porch—sweep and wash it thoroughly. Make sure any area that you're going to cover is very clean.

The turf usually come in 6' widths but you can get it in 12' widths. Purchase what you need. Measure out enough to cover the area to be covered. Get a utility razor knife and cut along the perimeter of the porch line. Once it is the right size, pick up the turf and roll back half of it. Spread your adhesive on that 1/2 of the porch surface being very careful not to get the adhesive up over the edge or on the sides of the house. Roll the turf back down again on top of it and do the same on the other side. This is a very easy process and most people can do it without much trouble.

The turf is excellent for knocking dirt, dust and particles off people's feet before they come in. It doesn't do a perfect job but it does help a great deal. It is easily cleaned by spraying with a garden hose.

I RECOMMEND that, in muddy areas or areas with a lot of moisture, you attach a scraper to your porch to scrape your feet before you enter the house. Doormats can be good or bad. They can be placed on top of the turf but don't rely entirely on a doormat itself to get the dirt off. You should keep your sidewalks clean leading up to your house or entrance areas coming to your house. Keep them swept and clean.

A NOTE ABOUT DOORMATS: When you purchase the door mat, try not to buy the black rubber type. So many of them when they get wet will stain the bottom of your shoes with black and as you walk on the carpet the stain goes down too.

Just inside the front door, you should have an entrance way where the carpet does not come right to the door. The carpet should be receded back 3' to 6' with an entrance that has a hard-surfaced floor on it, either vinyl, ceramic tile, or parquet. When you design your carpet layout, try to leave an entrance way of hard floors. The hard floors in themselves do not take the dirt off shoes but they provide an area on which to place an attractive throw rug to help take the dirt, moisture, or mud off the shoes.

In your kitchen, keep the floors scrubbed and clean. Use a washable mat in front of the stove that can be washed weekly or biweekly. Also make sure the floors of the kitchen are mopped and cleaned regularly so the grease does not build up.

If it is within your price range to buy a permanent waxed type floor, do it. We recommend you use these for your vinyl floors rather than the type you wax yourself. With a permanent waxed floor, the wax does not come up on your shoes nor does it come up with washings. It cannot be tracked onto carpeting. On waxed floors, the wax breaks down and will stick to the bottoms of your shoes and is tracked onto your carpeting, making the carpeting sticky and dirtier. Also available are permanent waxed tile floors or you may even choose to go ceramic tile. (However, see section on Ceramic Tile before you do).

Some people will use a plastic throw piece over their carpeting—clear plastic with tips to hold it in place. These are fine but only for temporary use. The main problem with the plastic is that the dirt concentrates on the edges of the plastic and as it concentrates, you get a straight black line on both sides of the plastic. In many cases it gets so concentrated that it becomes a permanent stain. This plastic also traps moisture underneath and this increases the possibility of mildew. Plastic on a temporary basis only, is fine.

You might also consider rotating your furniture. If you rotate it every 6 months to a year, this will help keep the wear of the carpet down and will help make the overall wear even throughout. Some rooms, I realize, are limited for moving the furniture around but where it is possible, rotate your furniture.

STAIRS

Stairs that are carpeted are always one of the first areas to wear out. If the stairway has been covered with the same type of carpet as the rest of the house, then this area will need more attention than most other parts of the house. The stairway takes more of a beating because of the constant scraping and shuffling of feet going up and down. You will have to keep this carpet very well vacuumed and free from all oil or grease build-up. If the stairs are anywhere close to the kitchen door, cleaning will be a nearly impossible task because the grease in the air from cooking will seek to rise. With stairs leading up to another level, air flow will also rise carrying grease with it, depositing it on the carpet as it goes. It's a never-ending battle.

Another help is the plastic runner. In this case it could be used permanently because, even with the disadvantages of plastic runners, it still is better than to have regular wall-to-wall carpet laid on the stairs without any protection.

In our estimation, though, the ideal situation for a stairway is to have the steps made out of hardwood and polished. Then use a regular carpet runner on the stairs. These are woven mats quite similar to the rugs that are put in expensive cars. They do wear like iron and are easily cleaned. They also can be installed so as not to be held permanently in place, with brass rods running across the width at the bottom of each step. This enables easy removal of the carpet for a more perfect cleaning.

CARPET WEAR AND PETS

How else can you keep your carpet looking good? You should not allow animals in the house. I realize animals are pets and usually part of the family but you have to bear in mind that if you are going to have a nice carpet you can't have pets on the carpets. It isn't just the fact that they may be totally trained and not have any inclinations of urinating on the carpet. Our main concern is that the claws of dogs and cats do rip the carpet. The claws of dogs walking in one area rips up the fibers and makes the carpet look pretty shabby after a while. (Pet Urine is discussed in detail in the Spotting section).

PETS— Dogs and cats also shed hair. This hair is very difficult to vacuum up even with the finest of machines. The hair also has a natural oil which gets on the carpet, not only spreading the oil and animal odor into the carpet fibers but it to will attract dirt.

FLEAS: The problem that plaques us all at one time or another. There are a variety of solutions for the occasional or minor flea problem. Flea collars, flea shampoos, sprays, powders and foggers. But its only the foggers of flea bombs that need to be mentioned in regard to your carpet. These automated sprays that you set off in the middle of a room, while you're out shopping do a good job of ridding the house of pests. But if they are used, the spray tends to accumulate on the carpet fabric and draws dirt to it, thus requiring an early cleaning. So you might take that into consideration when you plan to have the carpets cleaned. NOTE: In most states it is against the law for carpet cleaners to use any form of pest control in their cleaning methods or advertise that by cleaning your carpets it will eliminate fleas, or any other pest.

CARPET WEAR AND ADULTS

Do not go barefooted on your carpet. This is a mistake that many people make. Children, it seems are all right but adults have an oil on the bottom of their feet that definitely does stain carpets. As a matter of fact, the worse stained area in the home is the master bedroom. There is a definite trail from the bed to the bathroom. This trail, once it has been established with bare feet, cannot be removed very easily. It is a very difficult task to get this oil stain up.

We RECOMMEND you wear socks or slippers when walking on the carpet. Children do not emit this oil and do not seem to affect the carpet in this way, but adult bare feet definitely do wreck the carpeting.

Another problem that people are finding out about are the sponge rubber black soles that are on some shoes. When dry there is no problem, but just get them wet and you'll have tracks all over the house.

FURNITURE LEG IMPRINTS

Another problem many homeowners have with carpeting is that after they have left their furniture on their carpet for any length of time, they find imprints of the furniture left in it—holes from legs on the carpets leave deep gaps and most people don't know how to get these out. There are different ways to do this. To alleviate most of it, constantly rotate your furniture. But if the holes are there, use a kitchen fork and bring the pile back up with this fork. It's going to be bent over and it should be pretty permanent but it can be handled by using a wet washcloth. Soak it in hot water (not just warm but VERY Hot). Squeeze it out to damp but not dry. Place this hot washcloth on top of the area that you have just brought up with the fork. Then lightly massage the fibers with it. If you want to bring out your steam iron and use the hot steam squirting it on the washcloth that will also work but make sure you do NOT allow the steam to hit the fabric itself because it is too hot and will melt the fibers. I've made many repairs because of people laying irons on the carpet.

By using wide CASTERS, you can prevent these imprints from being left in carpets by heavy furniture. They come in many styles and types to fit the style of nearly every kind of furniture made today.

COASTERS TOO, are good to protect your floors from furniture legs and possible rust spots that may come from unexpected moisture.

CHAIRS WITH COASTERS

Although it is an excellent idea to have all your heavier furniture on coasters, it may not always be to your advantage to have small chairs on coasters. Not unless there isn't any carpet under them. Today many furniture manufacturers are making dinette sets with the table and chairs equipped with easy to roll coasters. It's a good idea unless your dinette set is on top of carpeting. Here's why. We have found in every incident of rolling furniture constantly back and forth in one area, that the carpet breaks down. This will happen even on a good commercial carpet or a rubber foamed backed carpet. The constant rolling will cause the separation of the primary backing from the secondary. Even if the pile doesn't start falling out, lumps will start to appear in the worn area and eventually it will disintegrate.

You may also find this happening under a desk where the chair is rolled back and forth.

To avoid this you might choose for the dining area not to have any carpet at all. Use a hard surfaced floor such as sheet vinyl. It's a lot easier to clean too.

Now if carpeting is a must, you may have your installer glue the entire carpet down in that room and use no pad. This type of installation is called Jute Direct, and is commonly used by businesses when insulation or comfort is not to be considered. By gluing the whole surface it will remove the need for a pad as far as it wearing out from the bottom side as discussed in the section on padding. But in time even this will not stop the carpet from deteriorating.

One other solution that is used in offices is the plastic mat. This mat is placed under desks and all areas that the person sitting at that desk may roll the chair. I'm sure you've seen these, and you may consider buying a large one for under your dining room table. They aren't that expensive and can be bought from anyone who sells office furniture or supplies. The only disadvantage to this again is the same problem that is encountered with plastic runners, accumulated dirt on the edges and possible mold or mildew because of moisture.

WRINKLES AND BUBBLES IN THE CARPET

We have already discussed wrinkling and bubbles in the carpet. This happens most often in moist humid areas of the country or whenever the humidity of a certain area is high and the carpet was not installed properly. Another reason this happens is that people drag heavy furniture across the carpet sometimes catching it on the carpet and pulling and stretching the carpet out of place. The wrinkling and lumps in the carpet, if they are not large or elongated, can be fixed simply by using hot water around the bubbles and wrinkles in the carpet. Do this only if the wrinkles are small. If they are large, you will have to have the carpet re-stretched. For the small wrinkles, get hot water, not boiling but near boiling, sprinkle it *around* the bubble to about 2 feet out from it. As the water dries, the carpet should shrink enough to take out the bubble or wrinkle.

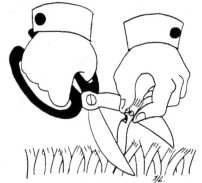

SNAGS IN THE CARPET

Another problem with carpeting sometimes happens when little pieces of carpet get snagged either on the bottoms of people's feet or when furniture is moved. These snags should never be pulled out by the fingers. Get very sharp scissors, gently pull the fabric up even and snug, then cut the snags off at the level of the carpet pile.

PREVENTION OF RUST SPOTS

Sometime during our lives we will come across the problem of rust on the carpet. This of course is caused from some metal coming in contact with your carpeting while moisture is present. This will usually be due to furniture legs that are capped with steel. Most floor lamps also have steel bottoms.

Your main protection from this of course is coasters placed under all furniture legs that have metal caps on the bottom. In years gone by nearly all furniture had these steel caps but today more and more furniture manufacturers are using hard plastic.

HINT: If coasters are too much trouble it might be wise to place a double thickness of aluminum foil under each leg.

Also if you are able to lift your furniture over on its side to check these steel caps, you might just replace them with new ones, if they are rusty. They are easily removed with a screw driver and hammer. New ones are sold in nearly all hardware stores, or variety stores and easily re-installed. (For removal of rust refer to RUST)

SOIL RETARDANTS

The soil retardants as mentioned in Part I will break down and there is no completely perfect method for using them again or renew it in the carpet like it was in the beginning. There are products available at janitorial supply houses that have a soil protection quality to them. As a matter of fact, you can even use a commercial starch which will actually waterproof and soil protect the fabric. I DO NOT RECOMMEND this for the non-professional. Not that he would likely hurt anything, but he may mix it wrong and end up with a very stiff carpet. You might want to try a spray starch lightly in the traffic areas. Be sure to let it dry thoroughly.

Beware of the unscrupulous carpet cleaners who will advertise soil retardant treatment, charging up to .12c a sq. ft. They come in and charge this after they have supposedly cleaned the carpet. Then what they do is use nothing but plain water and a garden sprayer. They go about the whole house spraying fresh clear water on the traffic areas and tell the people to stay off it for 5 hours. They sell this water as a soil retardant. This is not a common practice as most carpet cleaners are more honest than that but it does occasionally happen. The honest cleaners will at least attempt to give you what you have paid for. If a carpet cleaner offers the Scotchgard™ treatment, he should be licensed by the 3-M Company to use it 3-M is the Minnesota Mining and Manufacturing Company who invented Scotchgard" in the first place. There are others out on the market but 3-M is the only one that licenses certain cleaners to put it on carpets.

CARPET FADING

Today's carpets are dyed with colors that are permanent by all practical understanding of the word. But if a carpet (any carpet) is exposed to direct and prolonged sunlight, it will fade; so if an area of your house will have any direct sunlight shining onto the carpeting, it would be a good idea to close the curtains during that period of the day. Or have the windows tinted.

CASTERS THAT BLEED

Yep! Even though most casters are either glass or steel, some do come with a cloth fabric attached to the bottom. Now these casters are alright but don't allow the ones that have a colored fabric to get wet. (WHITE WILL PRESENT NO PROBLEMS). The dark colored ones will, when wet, stain your carpet and in all probability you will need some very professional help to get that stain removed.

FURNITURE THAT BLEEDS

With today's modern furniture you won't have the problem of the furniture finish, bleeding off into the carpet if it (CARPET) should get wet. But most furniture pre-1930 and nearly all furniture from the Orient and Middle East, will bleed. The reason for this is that the wood finish used on woods such as mahogany or teak, by the furniture makers of these lands, are usually oils and waxes. Plus some natural wood stains. They truly do leave a beautiful finish on wood but when the wood comes into contact with water it tends to separate from the wood and flow with the water. Some carpets are stained quite badly from this and here .again it takes major professional help to remove those stains from your carpet. Your best prevention is when your carpets are to be cleaned, have those pieces of furniture removed and not placed back on to your carpet until it is totally dried.

THOSE SPOTS THAT ALWAYS COME BACK

Nearly every household with a carpet down for any length of time has had the problem of a spot that would clean up but later would reappear. There are several reasons for this happening and at this point we will go into detail on why it happens and what you may do to prevent it from happening again.

Usually when dirt (not liquid) gets on the carpet, it will remain on the surface (the pile) of the carpet. At this stage, this is the time to get it up. If you do not manage to remove it by vacuuming, it works its way down to the fiber base and as time goes on and people continually walk on it, the very fine granules will work their way through the carpet (both primary and secondary backing) and then will be trapped between carpet and pad. To some extent this action cannot be totally avoided, but it can be hindered for years by frequent and careful vacuuming.

With this dirt now lodged between the pad and carpet, it is impossible to remove, short of taking up the carpet and removing the dirt. This source of dirt is a major reason for a spot that keeps coming back. It is not the only reason but none-the-less the major one. If that dirt was never to get wet it would do nothing more than lay there grinding up the secondary backing of your carpet so that eventually your carpet would fall apart. Keep in mind also that if dirt has worked itself through your carpet, it is also in between the first and secondary backing of your carpet. This dirt cannot be removed by any means and will continue to build up, also causing the carpet to fall apart and providing another source for dirt to stain the surface.

Here's what happens: Somebody spills something like water on the carpet. The water itself does not stain and won't hurt anything so you blot it up and forget about it. But as the carpet begins to dry the carpet gets darker. You see, the drying action of moisture rising will draw the color of the dirt up with it. This is very evident on light-colored carpets that have been poorly maintained.

The above is the action. Now I will explain some particulars that will go along with it.

If any type of oily substance is allowed to saturate through the carpet and is not removed at the initial spilling, then you will have a spot that will always come back. You can clean the surface over and over again but, unless you can get the source of oil out, it will come up every time the house gets warm.

Another source will be syrups and juices. As these saturate through the carpet, they add a stickiness to the dirt. This tends to draw the dirt together and concentrates it. Syrups and juices are not like oils which won't dry out. If it were possible to clean them up without getting the carpet wet, the stains would probably never surface again. However, to properly clean up a spill of this sort you must use water and as it dries, the stain again appears (see section on red berries—fruit juices etc.) back of book

Moisture from the floor—usually on concrete slab floors—is another reason for a dirty area coming back soon. This happens for a variety of reasons: anything from a broken pipe to a below-grade level floor. For minor moisture problems the floor can be sealed with a floor sealer. But what has happened is simply this. Rather than moisture being dropped on the top of the carpet, now it is seeping up from below. If the house is kept warm then it will get dirtier faster.

In this sense of the moisture coming from below, the stain may not even be caused from lack of proper vacuuming but it may even be from the old type felt pad. I've found on many occasions that the older felt pads will stain the carpet if they get too wet. It might be noted that the newer felt pads do not stain when wet but they will still hold a foul odor.

Another cause is usually in concentrated traffic areas such as the hallway, front and back-door areas, and in front of your favorite chair or couch. These are the major areas for build-up to work down into the carpet. It is also the area that will have to be cleaned two or three times when it is cleaned. This added attention to these areas adds moisture and, if that moisture is not taken out immediately, it will seep down into that trapped dirt again. As the carpet dries, that old dirt come up to stain again.

Another area that will cause a problem is that metal strip that separates the carpet from your hard-surfaced floors. Dirt builds up underneath that flap of steel and once it has worked its way underneath the only way to remove it is to pry up the metal and thoroughly clean out, wash and vacuum the carpet that was clamped underneath it. So often this area is more of a headache than the other areas because it will tend to get wet every time the hard-surfaced floor is washed. With this extra dampness the dirt area will spread and work itself out from the metal. See diagram page 50right hand column.

For areas of recurring spots caused from detergents, refer to section on SOAPS AND DETERGENTS.

PAINT THAT GARAGE FLOOR

A lot of dirt is tracked in from the garage area so not only do we suggest placing artificial turf at the garage door leading into the house, but also to paint the floor of the garage. WHY? Most garage floors are of concrete. This is usually not a sealed concrete and it is quite porous. You can sweep a garage three or four times in a row and get plenty of dirt up. You can even wash it over and over again, with the same results.

If you can, paint your floor with a good deck paint (any paint store will have it). Follow the directions and use two coats if possible. This paint fills in all those porous holes and gives the concrete a slick and easily cleaned surface. A good color is NAVY GREY. With that color the dirt won't hide. You might also consider the ease in which you can clean up oil drips from your car. Just a sponge and some gasoline and there won't be even a trace of oil.

One other thing we might mention for the garage. If you happen to have any large pieces of carpeting that was taken out of your house when the new carpet was put in, you might just lay them out in the garage. They will collect dirt and dust and also tend to help keep the garage warmer. Of course, oil will drip onto it from the car but if it's just a piece of throw-away carpet anyway, it doesn't make any difference.

VACUUMING

HOW TO GET THE RIGHT VACUUM CLEANER

THE DOOR-TO-DOOR SALESMAN

From time to time you will have the pleasure of having some stranger knock on your door—and guess what he's got for you? Yep! A vacuum cleaner. They always know when you've got to have one so they bring it over for your inspection.

After many demonstrations of showing you how you can paint the house, shampoo the carpet, take the wax off the floor, brush your teeth, and can vegetables—all with their vacuum cleaner—Oh, yes, and you can actually vacuum your carpet with it, too, they hit you with the price. After a pause and you have picked yourself up off the floor from being in shock, you will do one thing or the other: either, "Yes, I need help in canning my vegetables and therefore will buy it," or you politely show the stranger to the door.

If it's the door, he'll argue with you and show you how to put only a small amount down and just a little bit each month for the next twenty years to buy the best machine in all the world. He'll appeal to your emotions with, "Isn't it worthwhile to sacrifice a little now for the best? It will last a lifetime and the company has been in business since the pyramids were built in Egypt. So you know the product is an established name."

Again, you will do one thing or the other: you'll buy one for sure and maybe one for Mom for her birthday or you'll threaten to call the police if he doesn't leave. Threats don't phase him, though, because he's got one more "ace-in-the-hole"— THE FREE GIFT! "Yes, it's an all-expense paid vacation to Tibet in the winter time."

"Wow! You're kidding! I've always wanted to ski the Himalayas," you say. "Give me that vacuum and two more for my friends." After you've signed the contract and he's got you started cleaning the house while thinking about vacation plans you wonder, "Where did that wonderful Salesman come from?"

Where Do They Come From?

Usually the people who sell vacuums are just like anybody else except they're out of work, not working enough, or dissatisfied with what they're doing and want to try something NEW. And one day while looking through the Employment Section of the newspaper, they spot it—THE NEW CAREER OPPORTUNITY! It will read something like:

NATIONAL CO. NEEDS HARD-WORKING, Self-Motivated, Mechanically Minded Individuals for possible management positions to be filled in this area as soon as training is complete. For job interview, call JAKE SNAKE at 111-1000.

So he makes the interview appointment and naturally, there's a bunch of other guys down there trying to get the same job he wants. While he's sitting in this large room, the "Super Salesman" comes out and says all the right things about how they need good men. Then out comes "Super Salesman" number two and guess what he's got in the suitcase? Right, a vacuum cleaner. Out of courtesy, he sits there and listens.

Now Salesman #2 is really hot stuff and before long this poor guy is convinced he wants one of these things, too. Then he thinks of all the other people out there in the world who haven't had this "Golden Opportunity" to see this miraculous vacuum cleaner and if only he could show them. **"Wow!** How much money is to be made? If I could just sell one a day I'll be rich $ $ $ $."

So that's where they get their salespeople to sell their vacuums. A good salesman that does come along can get rich selling vacuum cleaners but the average of those that go anywhere with it at all is about 1 out of 20.

How About Their Product?

Is their product REALLY worth the money? That, of course, will depend on whether you use all the different attachments that you may end up buying. Remember, when you buy a new car, it isn't the standard straight car that the dealer is making a profit on—it's all the extras that you want with it. You know—bumpers, headlights, seats, steering wheel, etc. So also it is with these vacuum cleaners. If you buy just the basic machine, the dollars spent are about comparable with a store-bought item, just slightly higher.

IS THEIR PRODUCT REALLY THAT MUCH BETTER? They will say it is and, of course, the regular store-bought model salesmen will say they aren't. Who can you believe? My only suggestion is that you compare shop—look at price opposed to features and be sure you compare the GUARANTEES.

I've found that many extras are available on the private name brands that are not available on the store-bought items—one private brand uses a water filter system that is absolutely unique. It is especially good for people who are troubled with allergies and dust.

SO, WHAT DO I BUY?

For proper and sufficient vacuuming action, you should look for these features:

Group A

+ A ROTATING CLEANING BRUSH.

+ If it's an upright vacuum you should make absolutely sure that the dirt loads into the TOP of the dirt bag.

+ The handle must be able to tilt down—enabling the power cleaning head to get under furniture such as beds.

+ The power cleaning head should have a light up front.

+ The power cleaning head must have at least 3 different elevations on it to adapt to differing carpet heights.

+ Ease in attaching various cleaning tools.

Other features that are nice:

Group B

+ At least a 25 foot cord.

+ *A nice storage case that is easy to put attachment tools in and out of.*

+ A dirt bag that can be used over and over again—most vacuum cleaner manufacturers make a small fortune off the sale of replacement bags.

+ An edge-cleaning capability built into the power cleaning head.

All of the features in Group A may be found in most department store vacuums. At the time of this writing, May, 1980, you could expect to spend $80 to $ 130. On occasion, if you watch the specials, you may get it slightly cheaper.

When you start looking for more extras and additional power, then you will get into a higher-price range. If you're really looking for extras, then you'll have to go to the private brands to spend as much as $600—$700 for the works.

But again, I will remind you that all that is needed for a proper and totally sufficient carpet maintenance program is the features found in Group A. Anything above this is just a matter of preference and convenience.

HOW DO I USE WHAT I HAVE?

The vacuuming is the single most IMPORTANT ACTION that can be performed to increase the life of your carpet. If done properly and often, it will add up to 50% more life to your carpet. So it is important to learn the proper method of vacuuming and to stay on a disciplined schedule of frequent vacuuming.

FIRST, HOW DOES IT WORK?
AND WHY VACUUM AT ALL?

Although it is called a vacuum cleaner, it really is not a vacuum. The machine simply makes air to flow from a section of your floor into a retaining bag. Thus the dirt that is loose and in the section of the carpet that the machine is over will be lifted up when the air starts to move. The dirt with the air travels through a tube or channel until it drops into a bag. Most of the time the dirt will get stuck in the pile of the carpet and it needs to be brushed loose so as to get in the air-flow. This is accomplished by the rotating beater brush. It is very effective and will do an excellent job if the machine is moved over the carpet slowly.

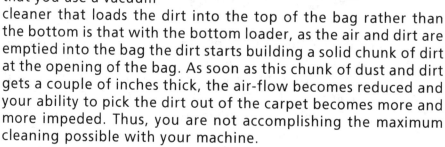

NOTE: The main reason we recommend that you use a vacuum cleaner that loads the dirt into the top of the bag rather than the bottom is that with the bottom loader, as the air and dirt are emptied into the bag the dirt starts building a solid chunk of dirt at the opening of the bag. As soon as this chunk of dust and dirt gets a couple of inches thick, the air-flow becomes reduced and your ability to pick the dirt out of the carpet becomes more and more impeded. Thus, you are not accomplishing the maximum cleaning possible with your machine.

The reason to vacuum is self-explanatory but here are some other reasons. Usually the dirt that does the most damage to the carpeting is sand, which is heavy and goes to the bottom of the pile. It takes quite a bit of agitation and a good vacuum to bring this up into the vacuum cleaner itself. So go over the area slowly, especially in the traffic areas. As often as 7 times in one spot.

Vacuum at least once a month every area of your carpet—around the edges and under the furniture. The reason for this is that we live in a society that pollutes the air. If you don't smoke, or have smokers in the house, the air will be a lot cleaner. There is a lot of dirt in the outside atmosphere which gets inside the house and naturally goes to the floor. It builds up and with grease forms a grit in the fibers. Vacuum this up as frequently as you can, going underneath all your furniture and around the edges at least once a month.

The main cause of carpet wear in heavy traffic areas is first the sand or little grits of dirt that get down and lodge down in the carpet pile. Glass is made from sand particles as you well know. Sand has many cutting edges on each little granule. If they lay loose in the carpet, there will not be much of a problem because they'll move around as you step on the carpet. But what happens is that the dirt and filth in the air today, and the grease, smoke and soot and everything else gets into the carpet. After awhile not only does the carpet have this film of dirt and filth on it but so do the sand particles. The sand particles start working like a snowball effect with the grease and grit. They become lodged and stuck to the fibers. As time goes by and sand and dirt particles are attracted into these areas, they stick together and form a real menace to the fibers. As you step on large chunks of this grit underneath, it will cut the fiber and then you start losing fiber because it is being cut from underneath as pressure is applied. That's why it is so important to vacuum these areas so thoroughly.

Also take great care in vacuuming over the metal strip that separates the carpet from your hard floor. Dirt will easily get trapped under that metal flap and, once it builds-up substantially, will start staining your carpeting as soon as it should get wet.

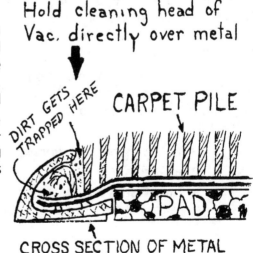

Hold cleaning head of Vac. directly over metal

DIRT GETS TRAPPED HERE

CARPET PILE

PAD

CROSS SECTION OF METAL

CARPET CRUSHING in the main traffic areas is another area of concern to most homeowners. A certain amount of this crushing can be expected but it can also be reduced by keeping it clean and frequent vacuuming and using a rug rake. On cut pile carpets, we highly RECOMMEND using the rug rake. Try to find a plastic-coated steel rake or, if not available, use a regular leaf rake. They are not very expensive and will certainly pay for themselves. In fact, for cut pile carpets (in the traffic areas), we RECOMMEND that you rake it up first before you start to vacuum. This knocks a lot of the dirt to the surface so that the vacuum doesn't have to work quite so hard on the fabric. After you have vacuumed, then you can go ahead and rerake your carpet. It makes the carpet look nice and keeps the tufts from sticking together.

Another way to minimize carpet crushing is to get a denser carpet, one in which the fiber is more dense. If it is possible, change the traffic pattern itself. Coming through doorways, this is impossible, but you can change the traffic pattern in the living room or bedroom by rearranging the furniture to spread out the traffic area.

NOW, LET'S VACUUM!

1. Don't plug it in yet.

2. First check the dirt bag and make sure it is not full. If it is, empty it or put on a new one. While the bag is off the machine, make a quick check at the connection point where the bag is attached to the machine. See that nothing is clogging that channel for a free-flow of air. Sometimes a bobby pin or toothpick will get lodged in there causing dirt to catch onto it and eventually building up a total blockage so that no dirt will pass.

3. Now, turn the machine over on its side and remove the steel plate that goes over the belt that is attached to the rotating brush. With you fingers, pull all hair and carpet shedding from off the brushes and from around the belt.

+ *this belt is made of rubber and will need to be replaced once a year,*

+ The brushes will wear down and should be replaced as they show signs of shortening.

Put the plate back on, making certain it is on tight.

4. Turn the machine upright and plug it in.

5. Use a slow forward and backward motion in the traffic areas. So often we see housewives vigorously vacuuming, moving the vacuum forward and backward as fast as they can. The truth of the matter is they are picking up literally nothing by doing this and not getting anything clean. They haven't been on any area long enough to get any dirt up from deep under.

6. Every 3-4 days go over the main living area lightly. For the average 3-bedroom house this entire operation should take about 1/2 hour.

7. Once a week concentrate on major traffic areas that lead to the outside or garage. Go over these slowly—allow 15 minutes.

8. Once a month, vacuum all areas that are possible to reach—under furniture and around edges—about 1 hour.

**** Total Time Spent Vacuuming Each Month: 4 Hours.
Time well spent since your carpet life will
be extended by 50% or more.

9. Empty the bag on your vacuum frequently. New carpet will shed a lot of fuzz and you are going to have bags full for several months at least. Watch for the empty mark on your bag and when it gets close to that line, be sure to empty it.

NOTE: A COUPLE OF HINTS.

+ Don't vacuum over your electric cord.
+ Don't try to pick up water with the machine unless it is made for that purpose.
+ Don't try to vacuum up large items that will not go through the machine.
+ Be sure to read the directions on the machine you buy.

MONEY-SAVING HINT ON VACUUM BAGS FOR UPRIGHT VACUUMS

Most stores that sell vacuum cleaners will without a doubt sell the various attachments, belts and bags needed for that machine. If you are following the suggestions in this book on vacuuming, then you will be replacing a lot of bags for your machine. Here is a hint on how to cut down on the COST of those REPLACEMENT BAGS for UPRIGHTS.

FIRST: While the bag is new, cut off the top.

SECOND: Put *2"* wide duct tape around the outside edges.

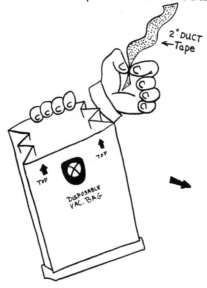

THIRD: Close up the bag and with 2" wide masking tape fold over the opening so that 1" of tape shows from both sides.

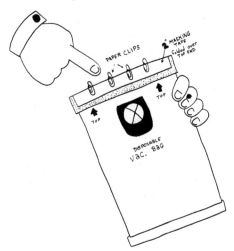

FOURTH: Take three or four paper clips and secure the bag shut. Refer to illustration.

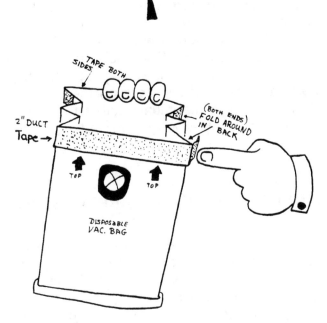

By doing this to your bags you may get anywhere from 5 to 10 uses out of each bag.

CARPET SWEEPERS

For years the carpet sweeper has been around and it is expected to be around for a long time to come. Its value is strictly in the eyes of the beholder. Its ability to clean up any ground-in dirt in a carpet is non-existent. But its value lies in the fact that it is lightweight, easy to get out and put away for those quick touch-up moments when guests are expected. Some will work as a quick sweeper for a hard surface floor. This could be a real timesaver. They are relatively inexpensive and almost never breakdown.

So if you want one for that cosmetic cleaning that so often is needed, have at it. But a word of caution. Some are not made very well and have tendencies to start dumping out dirt when they get too full, thus making a bigger mess than before you started.

HOW ABOUT THOSE BUILT-IN VACUUMS?

Some homes have a built-in system for vacuuming. Each room has a hole in the wall that is connected to a large and powerful motor. The housewife needs only to bring a hose and attachment around to each room and plug it in the wall and off she goes. These still must have a motorized beater brush attachment even though they have a more powerful motor that is creating stronger suction, they still must have the agitation of the brushes to get maximum results. Otherwise, the results are the same as for the portables and you've wasted a lot of money.

SHOULD I INVEST IN MY OWN CARPET SHAMPOOER?

There are some good shampooers on the market today but they cost quite a bit. The cheaper models won't really do for you what a rented machine can. If you can afford it, buy one. It will save you many dollars over the years and you might even be able to pick up a couple of bucks by doing the neighbor's carpets (or renting yours to them). A while back Sears was offering a steam cleaner that look pretty good. You might check on it.

DOES YOUR CARPET NEED CLEANING?

One complaint many people have is that they cannot understand why their carpet continues to get dirty faster once it loses its newness. It might take 3 years before it needs cleaning the first time and from then on out, it needs cleaning once a year. This is no big secret. It's just the fact that once your carpet is dirty, it's forever dirty. You will never ever get a wall-to-wall carpet clean again. Even the best cleaner can only get 60% to 70% of the dirt out of your carpet so you are always starting with a 30% to 40% residue. Originally your carpets may be treated with a thorough saturation of soil retardant. But once that retardant is removed from the carpet, the recurring soil increases much faster.

After you have your carpets cleaned the first time, you can be sure they will need cleaning more often and on a regular basis from then on.

The question that now comes to mind is, "How often should my carpets be cleaned once they reach this point?" This is up to you and the standard of living you maintain. Carpet cleaning, whether you do it yourself or have a professional do it, simply will not get all the dirt out, and it's not anybody's fault. It is in there to stay so you will have to live with it. There will be, as mentioned, a continuous residue of dirt left in from each previous cleaning.

If you have a heavy traffic area, you probably will have to clean the carpets before the end of the first year, but we have also had carpets that are cleaned every four years. It all depends upon the use and how well people take care of their carpeting.

Our advice is when you see the carpet looking a little bit shabby, and you have cleaned the stains and spots as they occur, go down and rent a machine to take care of the traffic area. Even if all you do is clean just the traffic area when it starts to show dirt and wear, this will help. Be sure to let it dry thoroughly before walking on it again. Moisture itself will draw dirt if you walk on it.

To determine if your carpet is really dry, stick your fingers in to the bottom of the pile. If both the base and surface are dry, then it will be dry.

An old myth is that the more often a carpet is cleaned the faster the carpet will wear out. This is entirely false in fact just the opposite occurs. The carpet will last years longer if it is properly maintained and cleaned regularly.

THINGS TO CONSIDER AND TO DO IF YOU'RE GOING TO CLEAN YOUR OWN CARPET

Many people start cleaning their own carpets and it takes them all day to do. This is only because they don't know the short cuts. We'll try to alleviate this now and make it easier for you to clean your carpet in 2 hours or less, depending upon what areas you want cleaned.

The first thing to do is pick a day that you can spend outside your house after you have finished so you don't walk on the carpet. Also pick a day when the sun is shining because the carpet will dry faster in hot weather than in rainy weather. Do it on a day when you can get some help. Many times professional carpet cleaners come in alone but they are trained and know what to do so they can handle a job that would normally take two people. You will need a helper if you plan to clean your whole house.

MOVE THE FURNITURE before you rent the machine. One reason homeowners have such a difficult time cleaning their carpets is that they don't know where and how to move the furniture around. This is not really a big problem. There is a little trick to it.

STEP1.   Remove all the small furniture items including everything that can be broken. Put them in the garage, kitchen, bathroom or wherever you can so they are off the carpet to be cleaned.

STEP 2.   Disconnect any stereo hookups and speakers.

STEP 3.   Remove books from any bookcases and move both books and bookcase to garage, or someplace out of the way.

STEP 4. Vacuum all the area you can see thoroughly. Don't bother going around the edges with edging tool at this time.

Make sure the vacuum cleaner bag is empty when you start and that the brush underneath the vacuum is cleaned off.

Pick up with your fingers all the small particles that won't vacuum up.

STEP 5. Move all the large pieces of furniture that are along the walls to a point that has been vacuumed, making a total switch so that everywhere you have vacuumed, there is furniture. This is usually accomplished by moving all the furniture towards the center of the room.

Its also at this point where you might consider rearranging your furniture to change the traffic patterns.

Vacuum those areas where the furniture was. Do this in all the rooms to be cleaned.

Bedrooms can be troublesome, especially with king-size beds, but it can be done.

STEP 6. After the furniture is moved and you have vacuumed, go around the edges of the carpet with the edging tool and the vacuum cleaner.

STEP 7. Make darn sure that all the edges of your carpet are securely down and that all seams are properly glued down. This is your best protection against any shrinkage.

STEP 8. Leave the furniture in the center of the room where it is. You will be cleaning open areas first and moving the furniture back after that in order to clean the inside areas.

STEP 9. Now, you're ready to start cleaning —well, almost. Go rent your machine for a minimum of 2-1/2 to 3 hours depending on your distance to the store.

STEP 10. If you haven't tried this machine before and don't know how it works or how fast to make it move and how to get the best results, DO A PRACTICE RUN FIRST in the driveway, kitchen or garage.

STEP 11. Mix some solution and practice for 15 or 20 minutes, moving the wand back and forth and shooting the water out. It is very important to feel comfortable with the equipment. See

what you can do with it on some grease spots in the driveway or garage. (This is for a steam cleaner. A rotary may be practiced with also in the driveway or garage.)

STEP 12. Proceed to next section on "How Do I Use That Carpet Cleaning Equipment."

SOAPS & DETERGENTS

These both have the same purpose—that is to remove soil, grease, etc. from a particular item which in our case is fabric. Although, technically speaking, soaps and detergents are not the same, we will for purpose of definition treat both cleaning agents as one.

The ability of these cleaners to perform their proper functions is in basically 4 major steps. I include these for your information so that as your carpets do get cleaned, you will understand the process by which the chemicals are doing the job of loosening the dirt.

THE CHEMICAL STEPS IN CLEANING

1. PENETRATION of the textile by detergent. Detergents will make water wetter, allowing it to penetrate and spread more freely.

2. ABSORPTION of the cleaning agent between surface to be cleaned and soil.

3. DISPERSION of dirt into a wash water or suds. This is accomplished by scrubbing and hot temperature. Much dirt can be removed simply by hot water alone.

4. SUSPENSION—Keeping the soil from once again attaching itself to the fabric. This is done by rinse or a vacuuming out.

NOTE: Some stains such as those of a protein nature (milk, blood, eggs, etc.) won't release to the detergent action alone. This is because they are not water soluble and penetration (step 1) cannot be accomplished. In this case use a detergent with ENZYMES to get the needed penetration.

This same process goes on in your washing machine as your clothes are washed but, because of the two-cycle rinse action on the machine, you generally aren't aware of the dirt being removed.

Also, when you wash your hair, you add soap, scrub, and rinse. However, as your carpets are being cleaned, this rinse action is not quite the same; in fact, it is usually non-existent. Although a good portion of the dirt is removed from the fabric by a powerful vacuum, the lack of a clean fresh water rinse action leaves much din in along with a residue of whatever detergent was applied. This one reason alone makes it so important to have a second person following you with a WET AND DRY VACUUM as you use a rotary method shampoo machine. The CLOSER he follows you the more dirt he will get up. In heavy soiled areas you may have to go over an area two or three times to get the majority of the dirt out. This also is a reason why we highly recommend ammonia to boost your cleaning power. It not only is death on dirt but it leaves no residue to later attract dirt.

With the STEAM CLEANING METHOD of carpet cleaning, here again there is no rinse action, but because the vacuuming process is immediate, as the detergent is applied, you will get out more dirt. However, if you buy a bad steam cleaning detergent, you will get more detergent residue than you want. This residue will attract dirt and your carpets will need cleaning more often.

With DRY FOAM-TYPE CLEANERS there also is not any rinse, but here again you have a quick recovery of dirt suspended in foam and scrubbed up. (With most machines of this type the recovery vacuum is not as powerful as might be used in the above two methods, therefore, leaving behind more cleaning solution residue.)

As you clean up spills on your own carpet, it is very important to get out whatever detergent you may have used by using clean rinse water and blotting up with a towel. Blot as much as needed until you feel all the detergent is out.

Very often people will get a stain out of their carpet quite effectively but, because they don't get the detergent out, they find a spot that keeps coming back to haunt them over and over again. If you do have something like this in your carpet and you have a professional come into clean, be sure to tell him about that spot. You see, if the recurring spot is because detergent wasn't properly washed out, the professional with his machine will go over it and it will come out temporarily, but unless he adds plenty of fresh water to rinse out the spot, that spot will come back again. He can't be blamed for this unless you tell him about it ahead of time.

NOTE: For other recurring spots, refer to THOSE SPOTS THAT ALWAYS COME BACK.

A BRIEF HISTORY OF
SOAPS & DETERGENTS

Soap has been known about for nearly 2,500 years and probably even longer. The Bible doesn't mention soap per se but in God's instructions to Moses on the building and functioning of His tabernacle. He gives instructions for a laver for washing purposes. This was done in the Area of Cleansing, after handling the animal sacrifices and burning of the carcasses. Since animal fat and ashes are the two ingredients in making soap, it is quite possible that the combination was used by the Hebrews to cleanse themselves. History tells us that the Hebrews were the cleanest people in all antiquity In fact. God's laws to Moses required frequent washings to keep the clean from the unclean. And if anyone would know how to keep things clean, it would be God. So I will assume that soap has been here a long, long time.

Over the years it has been traded between peoples as an article of barter. The Romans used it in all parts of their empire. In fact, the word soap is thought to have been derived from the Celts who named it "saipo."

During the middle ages soap factories sprung up in Marseilles, Genoa and Venice. Present knowledge indicates that soap was not in great use in the center of Europe but widespread on its borders. Soap making became big business as people learned to wash up before dinner and how to wash their clothes before they had to be burned (from the smell). And, of course, as production rose the bureaucrats found yet another item to tax. Things haven't changed much, have they? In fact, they taxed soap so much that they even put locking lids on the soap-boiling pans so that it could not be made at night and sold without a tax.

By the 19th century, though, the high use of soap had demanded that the tax be lifted and then someone decided that a nation's wealth could be determined by how much soap it consumed.

Progress in the manufacture of soap happened probably by accident at first, but by the 19th century soap making had become a science. As textile fibers went into the realm of man-made fibers, so also did soap. First as a crudely-made detergent developed by the Germans during World War I. This was done out of necessity because the Germans needed the available fats for other purposes (probably the storage of ammunition). This first detergent was called NEKAL, and although it is far from some of the modern detergents today, Nekal is still being made and used.

By the end of World War II, development of sophisticated detergents were well under way and in high production. One reason World War II produced such sophistication was because coconut oil was used in the finer shampoos and soaps; but as the Japanese took possession of the Pacific area that produced the coconut oil, we had to make other arrangements. Necessity is the mother of invention.

As it worked out, detergents were much better than soaps. Soaps would scum up in hard water -cause bathtub ring - visible residue- on glassware

HOW DO I USE THAT CARPET CLEANING EQUIPMENT?

We will discuss the two most popular methods only: the rotary shampoo and the hot water extraction (steam cleaning).

A. ROTARY METHOD: After you have properly prepared your house by vacuuming and moving the furniture as discussed in preceding section, you are now ready to start cleaning.

Stairs have to be cleaned by *hand,* then vacuumed; so have a bucket, hand brush, and hot soapy water ready.

-stickiness in rinse water - yellowing of laundry. Most of the problems were caused by calcium and salts found in hard water.

Detergents are hardly affected by the minerals in hard water; therefore, the problems were for all practical purposes eliminated. Detergents can also be soluble in cold water making them useful for cleaning purposes when hot water is not available.

BRIGHTENERS: This is a common additive that is incorporated into the making of modern detergents. Brighteners are dyestuffs that will be absorbed by the textile but once absorbed will not be rinsed out. HOW DO THEY WORK?

These dyestuffs change the invisible ultraviolet light (which is ever present during daylight hours) into a visible light on the blue color spectrum. This causes the fiber to reflect a greater amount of visible light. Thus it appears brighter.

NOTE: 1. Some detergents will contain abrasives—these are excellent for washing clothes but DO NOT USE AS A DETERGENT ON CARPETING! The reason for this is the abrasives are hard to remove without a thorough rinsing action that is not available.

2. SHAMPOO for carpets is either a detergent or soap. The act of shampooing your carpet is the act of applying soap or detergent to your carpet.

1. THINGS NEEDED

a. Tank-type rotary shampooer with scrubbing wheel or wheels.

b. One wet & dry vacuum cleaner with hose attachment and floor tool for carpets. (Can be rented).

c. Two people: one to operate shampooer, other to vacuum up the suds, water & dirt with the wet/dry vacuum.

d. Proper chemicals for cleaning. If you wish additional cleaning power to the chemicals you buy with your rental machine, a local janitorial supply store will have some plain ammonia you can purchase.

e. A hand spray bottle to put your ammonia and water mixture for pretreating spots, one part water, one part ammonia

f. If you have spots that may need a little extra to work up, then along with your spray bottle you'll need a soft bristle handbrush to scrub with.

2. PROCEDURES

a. Start in the farthest point into the house you can get. With the idea that you will want to work your way out to the front door without stepping on the damp carpet too much. If in a two story home, work backward toward the stairway.

b. Once in place, adjust handle of shampooer to slightly below your waistline. Now lay machine down and place scrubbing wheel(s) on the machine, making absolutely certain they are on straight and level.

c. Pick up the machine and lean it against some furniture at about the same angle it was when you lowered the handle to your waist. If there are any rubber wheels on the scrubber that will come up, now is the time to lift them up so that they are not touching the carpet.

d. Mix solution according to instructions. Add ammonia (1 cup ammonia to 3 gallons solution). At this time use your spray bottle mixed with ammonia and water and spray all spots that need that little extra touch. Then scrub lightly with the handbrush. Work only one room at a time.

e. Start at the farthest wall, moving to the *right.* When you have gone about 4 feet, go back over the same area to the *left,* all the time letting shampoo out with the control handle. CAUTION: Do not let so much out that you have a continuous flow as you move the machine back and forth. Only let enough shampoo out to leave a steady bead of foam.

f. After going back and forth 4 feet over the same path, come towards you with the machine 3 to 4 inches. Go right in a straight line again 4 feet, and back to the left again 4 feet. Move towards yourself again and repeat these steps.

Always remember to move the machine SLOWLY in all directions.

Your helper should be working either to your left or right. As soon as you complete a whole pattern back and forth, he should attempt to vacuum it up, *pressing down* hard on the floor tool to maintain maximum suction.

It sounds like it will take you an eternity but once you do a room or two, you'll get the hang of it and be finished in no time at all.

THINGS TO REMEMBER:

1. Put aluminum foil under the metal legs on furniture after you have finished. This prevents rust. spots on your carpet.

2. Plug each machine into different circuits, if possible. Otherwise you will blow a fuse. Example:

Plug shampooer in kitchen and wet/dry vacuum in bedrooms or living room. Kitchens are usually not on the same circuit as the other rooms.

3. When you're all done, try not to walk on the damp carpet for at least half a day. Take your spouse or family to dinner. Don't forget to invite your friend who helped you.

B. HOT WATER EXTRACTION (STEAM CLEANING) METHOD: This is not really steam but simply hot water injected into your carpet. If you actually put steam into your carpet it would probably fall apart or lose all of its color in no time at all.

The cleaning solution is run through a high pressure pump, down through the wand in your hand, and shot into the carpet. This hits the carpet fibers, knocking off the dirt and grease. Immediately, as this is being done, a strong vacuum is sucking the dirt and moisture right up into the waste tank. You have to empty this tank frequently and continually mix new solution as you do the carpet.

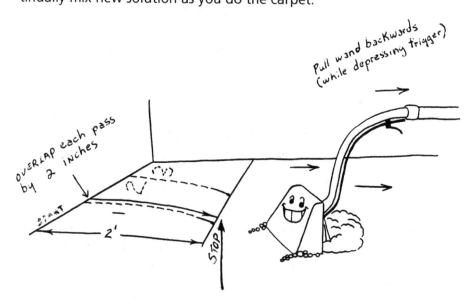

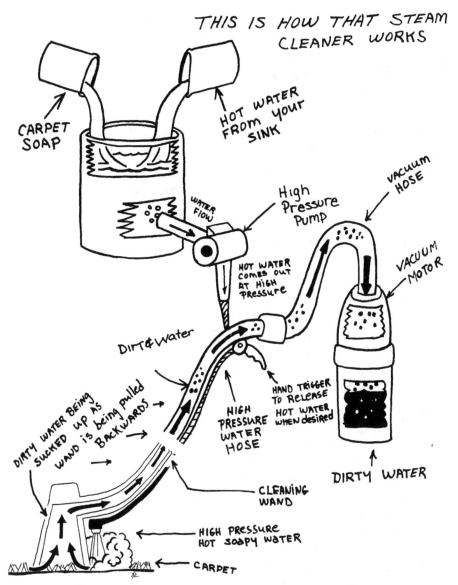

THIS IS HOW THAT STEAM CLEANER WORKS

CARPET SOAP

HOT WATER FROM your SINK

WATER FLOW

High Pressure Pump

VACUUM HOSE

VACUUM MOTOR

HOT WATER COMES OUT AT HIGH PRESSURE

DIRT & Water

HAND TRIGGER TO RELEASE HOT WATER WHEN desired

HIGH PRESSURE WATER HOSE

DIRTY WATER BEING SUCKED UP AS WAND is being pulled BACKWARDS →

DIRTY WATER

CLEANING WAND

HIGH PRESSURE HOT SOAPY WATER

CARPET

This method of cleaning is probably the most effective for the home-owner but it can be the most *destructive* method. This is not to scare you but to caution you. The reason people destroy their carpet is that they put too much water into the carpet and don't move the wand fast enough.

If for some reason carpet is not coming out as clean as you think it should, then after you have cleaned a section from front to back, then clean from left to right.

PROCEDURES ARE SIMPLE: Move the wand backwards across the carpet at a slow walk spraying while you walk. If the carpet is heavily soiled, move the wand slowly but not so slow the water begins to puddle up as you go. Don't spray while pushing the wand in a forward direction.

After each motion backwards—release the trigger and move the cleaning wand back over the area you just sprayed. Press down on the carpet to get maximum water recovery. Refer to illustration below for cleaning pattern.

These instructions are *in addition* to the detailed instructions that come in leaflets with your rented machine. Again, the cleaning solution that comes with the machine is not strong enough to do the best job so add ammonia (1 cup ammonia to 3 gallons solution.) for that additional cleaning power.

Of course, you are interested in calculating whether or not it is worth it to rent one of these machines or call in a professional. That is a decision you will have to make based on how much you want cleaned. You are usually doing this kind of thing on your day off and spending anywhere from $8. to $45. in carpet cleaning equipment plus all the chemicals you'll need.

If you do plan to clean your entire house and if you have, tor example, a three-bedroom house with living room dining room, and hall all carpeted, your savings would be great. Some rental steam cleaning machines come with a small hand-size cleaning wand that you can use on your stairs. This is a very convenient tool, and it certainly makes the cleaning of stairs easier. They suggest also that you can use it on your furniture. If you should decide to try to clean your furniture, please don't try it with anything expensive or valuable. Even the most experienced professionals have ruined furniture on occasion. The proper cleaning of furniture is nearly a science and involves much more than does the cleaning of carpets.

One interesting machine that has come out in the last few years that you may be able to rent is the RUG DOCTOR™ with the vibrating brush. If you can find it, it will do you the best job of any rental carpet cleaning equipment. It not only has the usual steam cleaning method of operation, but it incorporates a brush that moves back and forth across your carpet, scrubbing as it goes, and it is effective. This machine, however, is not that available and may be hard to locate. It also costs more to rent.

With any machine that you rent you will receive written instructions on the operation of that particular machine. They will also want you to buy their particular products for operation in their machine. Its actually in the sale of those products that they make their big money. The chemicals usually offered are rated from fair to good. None are of real professional quality regardless of what is printed on the side of the container. I'm not saying that professionals don't use those products. It's just that a lot of "professionals" aren't professionals and really don't know what they're using.

These machines will all require that you use a "DE-FOAMER" of some kind. This is very IMPORTANT. Without it you would probably have to empty the machine every couple of minutes. The de-foamer will make the foam or suds that are being sucked up out of your carpet dissolve, thus allowing more room in the waste recovery tank for dirty water. This gives you more cleaning time before you have to empty.

Some machines have the waste tank that will come out like a bucket, which is very convenient. A hint on keeping suds down would be to take a small handful of lard and spread it around the inside of the bucket. You might also use lard that has been partially melted. Then let it be sucked up the vacuum hose. This action will coat the inside of the hose and also reduce the foam build-up. This method of defoaming is cheap and very effective. Not much is really needed, and you can always use the rest in your kitchen. But keep in mind that the defoaming action is required from time to time during the entire cleaning operation, but still you won't use much.

If you are not satisfied with the cleaning chemicals supplied with the machine, you may want to go to a janitorial supply and get some professional strength chemicals. It should be noted, though, that if you find more strength is needed you can just add straight ammonia (1/2 cup) to each cleaning solution you mix. This will add more cleaning power. NOTE: Be certain not to use anything but pure ammonia (a concentrated ammonia is available at any janitorial supply house).

SUGGESTED FURNITURE MOVING PLAN FOR THE BEDROOMS

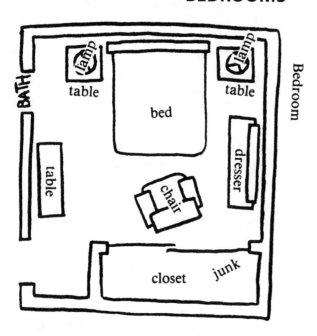

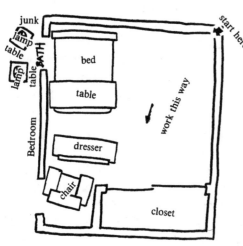

REMEMBER TO START CLEANING AT THE FURTHEST POINT FROM THE FRONT DOOR, AND ALWAYS WORK BACKWARDS.

STEP 1.

MOVE ALL FURNITURE AS FAR AWAY FROM YOUR STARTING POINT AS YOU CAN.

STEP 2.

CLEAN ALL EXPOSED CARPET

(include closets

always)

STEP 3.

MOVE FURNITURE OVER TO SIDE OF ROOM THAT HAS BEEN CLEANED, AND CONTINUE TO CLEAN THE REST OF ROOM. (Don't do hallway until all rooms *off of* the hallway have been cleaned.)

STEP 4.

PUT ALL FURNITURE BACK INTO ITS ORIGINAL POSITION. PLACE TIN FOIL UNDER ALL FURNITURE LEGS THAT HAVE METAL CAPS.

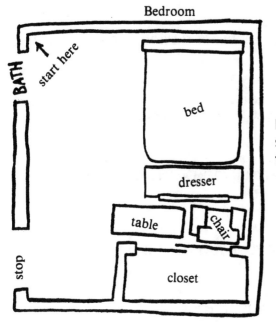

NOTE: You might leave all small items off *from* the floor until totally dry.

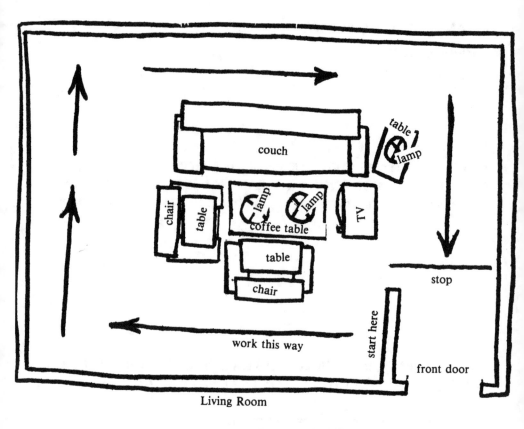

Living Room

1. FURNITURE SHOULD BE IN THE MIDDLE OF THE ROOM AFTER VACUUMING.

2. AFTER THE OUTSIDES OF THE ROOM HAVE BEEN CLEANED THEN PUT FURNITURE BACK WHERE YOU WANT IT. (This is a good time to rearrange.)

3. DON'T FORGET TO PLACE TIN FOIL UNDER EACH PIECE OF FURNITURE THAT HAS METAL CAPS ON THE LEGS.

4. CLEAN THE CENTER AREA ON YOUR WAY OUT THE FRONT DOOR.

5. STAY OFF FROM THE CARPET UNTIL IT IS DRY.

ODORS & DEODORANTS

Over the years your carpet may acquire an unpleasant odor which may not be noticeable to you. It builds up so slowly that your sense of smell becomes immune to it. The best way to find out if there is an odor problem in your house is to ask a friend. Make sure they understand you want the truth; otherwise, out of kindness, they'll say that everything is fine.

Where do odors come from? There are as many sources for bad smells as there are fibers in your carpet, but there are some primary sources: pets, smoking, food spills & cooking odors, and residual moisture.

1. PET ODORS (NOT URINE) are present because the animal has not been washed. Did you know that animals have body odor? Now it isn't the general practice of pet owners to give a squirt of Ban Basic under the legs of their pets so if you don't bathe them regularly, they will begin to have an odor. Of course, this odor is passed from fur to carpet, furniture, and drapes. This pertains mostly to dogs. The older the dog becomes, the stronger the odor, so more frequent washings are in order. Some flea powders have a mild deodorant added which does help.

Cats, on the other hand, although they too have a body odor, are not nearly as potent. Cats just keep themselves cleaner by nature. However, the source of cat odor in the home will come from the litter box. This box should be changed regularly and a deodorized litter used. If you want an alternative to this, use clean sand mixed with baking soda. Mix it 1 cup of baking soda to every ten pounds of sand. Whether you use the bagged litter or sand, make certain that you put clean newspapers in the bottom of the catbox each and every time. When you empty the box, wash it out with a strong detergent *every* time. The odor from a catbox can permeate a household in a very short time. It not only gets into the carpeting, furniture, and drapes, but if you have an acoustical ceiling, it will penetrate even that.

2. SMOKING ODORS are the second greatest cause of foul odors in the home. Not only does smoking leave a bad odor but it leaves very visible evidence. In homes where smoking is the practice you can expect to have everything cleaned at least once a year to get rid of these odors. If you don't, then you may see drapes turning orange-brown, furniture becoming sticky, and the ceiling turning dark yellow. (If it is an acousti-cal ceiling, it must be painted to cover over the color and smell.) The carpet, of course, is like a magnet to odors and will reflect the smoking habits of the household.

If there is smoking in your house and you wish to see how serious the build-up is, wipe your finger across the top of your curtain rod. If what is on your fingers is dark yellow or orange-brown, you can get a good idea of what is in the carpet, furniture, and ceiling.

Avoiding this odor is easy—don't smoke in the house.

Today, at an every increasing rate, more and more people are smok-ing marijuana. This also leaves a foul residual odor which is even more repugnant than tobacco smoke. Keep in mind that it is much more difficult to get rid of marijuana odors, although both leave very foul odors over prolonged use. Incense has been used to cover the smell of marijuana smoke, but it is only effective during the initial smoking. We are stressing the residual odor and the *only* way this can be eliminated is not to have it present in the first place.

3. FOOD ODORS from cooking fortunately will not have a lasting effect except in the exact location of the cooking operation. The smell of foods such as garlic or onions doesn't remain in areas that are in other rooms. Your main concern then is around the cooking and food preparation area.

To avoid lingering odors, don't have carpeting in the kitchen. Adequate ventilation is necessary. Use your stove fan and, if necessary, open a couple of windows for cross ventilation. Clean all surfaces regularly.

What about those food spills? These are always accidental and are going to happen. When you have spills, clean them up immediately. Refer to the back of this manual for exact instructions to follow for spills on carpets.

4. MOISTURE is also a major cause for odor, especially from toilet overflows. For complete information about moisture in your carpet, refer to the section on *Floods* (Minor Floods).

For URINE ODORS refer to back of book on URINE.

SO WHAT, I'VE STILL GOT ODORS!! Ok, so you have odors and you want to know what to do about them. Start with an overall cleaning of everything. If you can afford it, have your carpets and drapes cleaned first by professional cleaners. Specify to them that you want the carpets and drapes deodorized.

As your budget permits, have your furniture cleaned. This is usually more expensive than even having your carpets cleaned, but by having them cleaned professionally, it will be done right and they will be deodorized properly.

The rest you can do yourself. Clean all surfaces, ledges, hard furniture, hard-surfaced floors, windows, bedspreads, cupboards inside and out, and all bathroom and kitchen fixtures. This will get rid of most odors, but you still may have to paint, especially if smoking is permitted on a regular basis. After these steps, if the odor persists, you may have to refer to section on *Floods* or on *Urine.*

POWDERED DEODORANTS FOR YOUR CARPET

These products have been tested and used for a number of years. We have determined them to be effective in reducing odors from carpets. Even in severe cases of odor, they have reduced to some extent the foul-smelling air in a closed room

The most effective way to use these powdered deodorants is:

1. Vacuum thoroughly all areas to be sprinkled with powder.

2. Sprinkle powder evenly but abundantly in the desired area.

3. Use a broom and spread the powder around and into the carpet pile.

4. Leave for 2-3 hours and don't walk on it.

5. Vacuum very thoroughly until no trace of powder is left.

One thing to keep in mind, however, is that the powder is only a temporary means to keep odor smells out and cannot be looked upon for any permanent solution to odor problems. While powdered deodorants are quite effective with minor odors, they will not entirely eliminate severe odor problems.

It should be noted that not enough testing time has passed to determine if the residual powder placed on the carpeting will cause faster soiling. At this time this has not been found to be true.

POTTED PLANTS ON THE CARPET

More people totally destroy the carpeting underneath where they place potted plants. If you have plants, use a spill plate underneath the pot itself. A spill plate is a plate that retains the overflow moisture from watering. This, in itself, is not enough. Moisture has a way of working itself through waterproof substances. So get the pot and spill plate raised up by some means to allow a free air flow underneath. Hanging plants are ideal but some large plants are quite attractive on the floor. May we suggest a finished piece of redwood or cedar the size of the spill plate or a little larger. Attach casters to the bottom. Not only is your carpet protected this way, but if you decide to redecorate, you can just roll the plant to a new location.

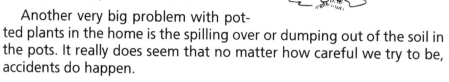

Another very big problem with potted plants in the home is the spilling over or dumping out of the soil in the pots. It really does seem that no matter how careful we try to be, accidents do happen.

SO WHAT DO YOU DO? If the spilled dirt from the plant is still wet from a recent watering, DO NOT USE YOUR ROTATING BRUSH VACUUM!

Pick up the spilled mud with a spoon as much as you can. Do not rub or scrub this area. Most potting soils have a pigment in them that will, when wet, transfer the color of the mud into the carpet fiber. It is not a permanent stain but if you follow these precautions it will not be any worse than necessary. Let the mud dry completely. Stay away from it until it is dry and dusty-like. If water spilled out with the mud, then place paper towels over the spill area pressing down lightly until moisture has been transferred to the paper towel.

Once the mud has dried, it is time to vacuum. If you do not have any attachments for your vacuum cleaner then clean as best as you can. But if it is at all possible to get an edging or crevice tool, use it in this manner:

1. Turn the vacuum on holding the tool in your right hand.

2. Place your left hand on the carpet, bending over the pile and exposing the primary backing and the dirt.

3. Vacuum this up, moving your left hand ever so slowly exposing each new area so that the suction from your vacuum may remove it.

This process, of course, would be done on all areas of carpeting that would have a large build-up of dirt (entryways, etc.).

After the initial vacuuming, use water mixed with ammonia (1 part ammonia to 3 parts water) and wash out any dirt stain left. Blot it dry with a paper towel and stay away from it until it has thoroughly dried. Anytime your carpet gets wet, do not put any object over the damp area until it is dry.

FLOODING

A. SEVERE FLOODS

In the past this subject would not have to be mentioned because people in flood areas knew what to do about their floors. But today as the weather changes more each year, new people are experiencing flooding for the first time in their history. A good example of this is the recent floods in southern California. Nobody was ready and most people lost everything that the waters touched.

There are some guidelines you can follow in the course of rising flood waters. The most obvious, of course, is don't live in flood plains at all. The oceans and rivers will always claim their own. It may take

100 years or more but it will always happen. If possible, live on high

ground. I know that this is rarely possible as people have to live in places they can afford and which are the most practical.

With this in mind, these instructions will be to those who live in a flood area and who have sufficient time to prepare—at least 1 day— before the water level reaches your floor level. If you have a second story on your home, you're in good shape: you can just move everything upstairs. If your home is only one story, follow these steps:

1. Put all important papers and valuables in your car if you are leaving.

2. Gather up sleeping bags, pillows, blankets, and several changes of clothing for all family members and also put in the car.

3. Disconnect electricity at box.

4. Turn off gas and water.

5. Take up carpet and pad in the largest room of the house. Refer to step 8 for instructions on how to take it up.

6. Move all small items to the attic or counter tops. Move all large furniture to the largest room. Use tables with legs as supports for easy chairs. Place all upholstered furniture on top of tables and furniture that are not upholstered.

7. Remove all dresser drawers and put in attic or up on shelves. Then use as many pieces of furniture as necessary to hold the mattresses. If at all possible, get everything *at least three feet* off the floor. This includes your drapes also. Take clothes hangers and put the drapes through them, then hang them up to the curtain rod.

8. REMOVING THE CARPET: After everything else is up, take the rest of your carpet up. This is done by first using a razor knife to cut the carpet in as straight a line as possible in every doorway (not closet doors) where the carpet goes through the door into an adjoining room.

In the places where the carpeting stops at the kitchen floor or bathroom floor, you will usually find a metal strip. If you don't find nails through the top of it, you may insert a screwdriver between the metal and the carpeting and pry up the metal. If no metal is visible just pull up hard on the carpet and it will come out.

If the metal has nails or screws down through the top, use a claw hammer to pry this up first.

After the carpet has been cut and the metal lifted, go around the edges, lifting up the carpeting by pulling it off the tack strip. Be careful not to get too close to the tack strip. The nails will cut and rip your skin.

After the carpet has been loosened, roll it up and tie it. With some help from your family or neighbors, place the rolls up on anything that will hold the weight.

If you have any space left, you may try to salvage the padding that was underneath the carpet.

What happens if the water level rises above the three-foot level in your home? This is always a possibility, but it usually is not the case.

You might ask, "Why not get a truck and move everything out?" This is the ideal solution. However, if you don't own a truck personally, the chances of getting one are quite slim, especially if you are in an area where hundreds of families are being flooded. There just aren't enough rental trucks available.

OUR RECOMMENDATION is, if you live in an area where you even think there may be a flood, go ahead and make preparations for it. Buy 3 or 4 sheets of plywood, 4' x 8' x 1/2 "; and when the threat of flood is imminent, place those boards over tables and chairs, making a huge platform on which to place all the other items. Also keep a razor knife, twine, screwdriver and claw hammer easily accessible.

We all hope that a flood never hits; but, in the event of one, at least you have some ideas on how to salvage most of your valuable items.

NOTE: Remember that with a flood, it isn't the water that causes the major damage—it's the mud and silt. If things just get wet they can dry out, but mud and silt can never be cleaned out of carpets or upholstered furniture.

When it comes time to install the carpet again, have a professional do it if it is within your means.

If the carpet does get soaked with water, but not saturated with mud, spread it out anyplace you can, lifting it off the floor or ground to allow air to circulate both underneath and on top, until it is dry.

B. MINOR FLOODS

Minor floods are by far the most desirable if a flood must happen. These are caused by such things as toilet overflows, leaking water heaters, or just accidents with large amounts of water.

To avoid this from happening is next to impossible. The only safeguard is to keep your water heater on a lower level than you floor level. You might also take certain precautions with your water heater on a lower level than your floor level. You might also take additional precautions with your water heater. Drain it out at least twice a year, and every couple of years have an inspector from the utility company come out to inspect it for possible signs of wear. You might also call a plumber but his fee will be far more than the utility inspector. Some utility companies will make the inspection free, so check it out. It's well worth the effort to get it fixed before it floods your house.

With toilets, there is only one thing you can do to help prevent over-

flows: Call a local drain service to clean out your sewage line every two years; and from time to time, use a drain cleaner. Most people don't know that regular use of a drain cleaner actually does help to keep that muck from building up. However, drain cleaners won't get out roots. Only the drain service man can do that.

Another precaution is don't put things down the garbage disposal that don't belong there such as grease, onion peels, celery, etc. When you wash your hair make sure you have a screen over the tub drain. Most hardware stores and supermarkets carry them. Human hair is one of the primary causes for clogged drains.

When you turn the water on someplace in the house, make sure you don't go off and leave it running. If the sink is partially clogged (drains slowly) it will overflow before it drains out.

Ok! So you've taken all the precautions and the TOILET OVERFLOWS. WHAT DO I DO?

1. Stop the water flow into the bowl: take the top off the toilet tank. Reach inside and put that rubber flapper down so that it covers the hole. The tank can refill safely as long as the hole is covered.

2. Get old rags and towels and lay on the floor. Use as many sponges as you can get as fast as you can. The longer the water is on the floor, the further it will penetrate into the carpet and pad at the doorway.

3. The bathroom floor is now dry and cleaned up. If you acted fast enough, it won't be necessary for you to do anything else except to use a plunger on your toilet.

4. If the water was dirty (sewage) water and it got into the carpet, you will have to lift it up to let it dry out. If the water was clean water and did not get the carpeting very wet, just place a towel on the wet carpet, press down with your foot, and do this until very little moisture is shown in the towel. This should be sufficient and all that is needed.

In the event of dirty water, you must pull the carpet as far back from the entry as it takes to expose the entire wet area. This may require cutting with a razor knife as described in Step 8 of *Major Flooding.*

5. After this is done, you will probably have to replace the padding underneath. Using the razor knife again, cut around the wet area, making your cuts straight so that you cut out a square or a rectangle.

Take this padding to the dealer where you bought your carpet, if possible, and ask for a piece of the same type and weight. He may give it to you for free. If you don't know where the padding was purchased, go to any carpet store and buy a small piece.

NOTE: If you had padding installed at the same time as your carpet, save the large scrap pieces of padding and carpet for just such emergencies as this.

6. With your razor knife, cut the pad to fit but don't put it down until the floor is completely dry. Wash the floor and use a spray disinfectant. Spray also the back side of the carpet. Now place the piece of new padding into the spot and tape it to the old pad with masking tape. If you can get DUCT TAPE, this is even better. Tape all the edges that are touching the old pad. This is done to keep the pad from separating underneath. Sprinkle BAKING POWDER onto the pad before you lay the carpet. This absorbs odors.

7. After the carpet has dried (you may want to speed this process up by using fans or electric heaters), it is now time to place the carpet back down. If the wet area was very large and your carpet was not totally synthetic, it probably did shrink and you should call a professional.

However, if it was a small area, you can do it yourself. If you had to cut the carpet when you lifted it, refer to the back of this book under the title, *"Repairing and Making Your Own Seams."*

After your seam has been made and allowed sufficient time to dry, now with a firm grip on the carpet with both hands on the edge that will go directly in the middle of the door, push it forward up over the wooden tack strip until it catches.

Work the rest of the carpet up onto the strip until it is all on the tack strip and flush to the wall and to the metal in the doorway. You may have to push the carpet with your hands until it gets close enough to the wall.

Take a stiff-edged putty knife or an old butter knife and place it on top of the carpet that is over the wood tack strip. Using the flat edge, press down, and move the knife over the carpet, forcing it down onto the tacks. Go over it several times until you're sure the tacks are in securely.

In the doorway where the metal is, tuck the carpet into the metal fold and use a hammer to beat the metal down.

If you do this job yourself, you will save $25 to $65.

NOTE: As a final touch, put some powdered carpet deodorants down according to directions under *"Powdered Deodorants for Your Carpets."*

FINDING A PROFESSIONAL CLEANER

The professional carpet cleaner is one that you can either trust with your life or you have to watch every move that he makes, never knowing whether he's doing the right job. I'm not trying to put a smudge on the industry with this statement but the unfortunate truth is that there are a lot of crooks out there who are disguised as carpet cleaners.

The bona fide carpet cleaning men are generally owner/operators. They own their own business and operate it. They are very much concerned about whether they get repeat business or not, and about making sure the job is done properly to your complete satisfaction.

There are various carpet cleaning organizations around the country that have a very good reputation for making sure their members are men of integrity, honesty, and professional enough to handle most of the problems that come up with carpet cleaning. They have seminars, cleaning conventions, and are constantly trying to stay up with the industry—developing new methods and chemicals to deal with today's dirt and carpet problems. Between 15% to 30% of the carpet cleaning force today belong to these organizations. That doesn't mean that the rest of the carpet cleaners are not good, honest businessmen just because they don't belong to an organization. I operated 8 years without belonging to an organization but I can certainly appreciate their worth. The only reason I didn't join was that my teachers were teaching them. I was very much up on the industry and stayed up on it all the way through.

However, the truth of the matter is, that the majority of people in the carpet cleaning industry are NOT up on it. They basically have a little more knowledge of it than you do. They come into your home with machines which they don't even know how to operate. They will scrub, scrape, rip, and do all kinds of things to your carpeting and then tell you that is the best that anybody can do and for you to pay them.

We've seen terrible destruction done by these men.

The carpet cleaning industry is extremely technical and sophisticated. New problems arise all the time, and new methods have to be derived at to solve these problems. It isn't like the old days when you could just call a janitor who would come and get your carpet, pick it up and take it down to his shed, shake it out, and vacuum and beat it. Then he would pour gasoline on it and wash it with the gasoline and you would have a dry cleaned carpet. Those days are long gone.

Today's carpet cleaning machinery costs upwards of $5,000 to $35,000 Just for the machinery to clean your carpet. (This is not just a scrubber and vacuum like many cleaners use but powerful truck-mounted machinery that REALLY WILL CLEAN your carpets.)

I wish we could tell you who is the best carpet cleaner in your area, but since there is no way to do this, there are some guidelines you can go by.

The number one guideline is "WORD OF MOUTH." Have your friends had somebody in recently who did a decent job and they were satisfied with the job and price? Don't go looking for bargains, please. There are no bargains in the carpet cleaning industry.

If you find an ad such as, "We'll clean 5 rooms for $24.95", then there is something fishy somewhere. A group of people in Southern California have been putting out these ads for some years and the only reason they stay in business is because California is a high transient area. They would never survive in a city without a high transient population. In Southern California the average housing turnover is 3 years.

Unscrupulous businessmen are much easier to find in the cities and transient areas than in the rural areas where people are settled and know each other. Since most people live around the cities, this is what we are dealing with. These ridiculously low prices in ads are a come on. They come into your house with equipment that you can rent yourself at the grocery store rather than anything with any real power. They use the same type chemicals that you can buy. When they are all finished, they have done a lousy job and have usually charged much more than their advertised price.

I was personally called in on one job where this outfit had advertised that they would clean the living room and hallway for $15. They came out to this little old lady's house (for real) and moved all the furniture out in the front yard and cleaned her carpet. She wasn't too happy with the results but how could you complain for $15? Actually it was $14.95. As they started to leave, she asked, ^Aren't you going to move my furniture back into the house?" They said that would be an extra charge. They ended up charging her $30 for the whole job because she was alone and they knew she couldn't get any help. She was helpless. The carpet didn't dry properly and wasn't properly cleaned so she called us at the urging of her neighbor. We had to redo all the carpet. It was a sad situation.

In other incidences, outfits have charged for everything you can think of. They call it preconditioning, pre-spotting—extra charges. Your carpet may only need light touch up but they convince you to have a thorough deluxe carpet cleaning job done by the most expensive chemicals they have. They will advertise to clean your house for $19.95 and end up walking out with $60 or $75. These outfits are eventually caught. One is presently under investigation in one of the northern counties of California with three multiple charges levied against them. If more people would speak out against these people, they would certainly be put out of business quickly. This goes on in any city. These things are mentioned, not to be negative and scare you out of having a professional cleaner do your work, but mainly to alert you that there really are some crooks in the business. Most people don't speak because they are ashamed and don't want to admit they were taken. Nobody wants to admit they were fooled; so for such a small monetary loss, they don't squawk too loud.

There are several professional methods of carpet cleaning and you have to decide which method you want for your carpets.

One of the oldest methods of cleaning is the dry foam cleaning. It comes under various names and usually they are a franchise operation. Ask when you call which method the cleaner uses. These dry foam cleaners do have some advantages. They are good for high traffic areas such as airport terminals which simply cannot close down for cleaning. They do the job fast and leave the carpet almost totally dry.

There is a DISADVANTAGE to the dry foam cleaner. They don't get the carpet that clean. It is OK for areas that are maintained on very short, regular intervals where there is high traffic. It is not effective for a very soiled carpet. We do not recommend the dry foam cleaning for the home. You can get a much better cleaning job for the same price or less through other methods.

THE ROTARY SHAMPOO METHOD: Also a very old method of cleaning. It takes two men to do the job effectively—one runs the shampoo machine, the other runs the wet/dry vacuum behind him sucking up suds and moisture almost immediately after the shampooer puts it in. This is the most effective way to run a rotary shampoo operation.

The brush (or brushes) rotate in a circular fashion breaking down the dirt and oil that is built up. Immediately the wet/dry vacuum is used to suck up the suds, dirt and grime.

One way to determine how good the job is done is check to see that the carpets are not over soaked and there are no streaks left. Streaking is a sign of 2 things: Either they didn't know how to use their machines properly; or, even if they did know how to use their machine, there was so much dirt in the carpet that it turns to mud. Once the carpet has so much dirt it turns muddy, your best bet is to throw the carpet away and buy new carpet. We rarely see this, however. Most people have more respect for the carpet and do not allow this kind of buildup.

If you should move into a house where there is a great deal of dirt embedded into the carpet already, especially in the front door areas and areas of entrance onto the carpet, you can feel with your fingernail and tell if it is packed full of dirt. If it is, the chances are you are never going to get it clean and you will be much better off replacing the whole thing.

If money is a problem for total replacement of the carpet, you might call in a qualified floor covering installer and have vinyl put down in your entryways. It is usually the front-door, back-door and garage-door areas that will have built-up dirt so bad that you can't vacuum it all out.

Also in areas of high dirt build-up, use the method of vacuuming described in the carpet section on POTTED PLANTS.

THE STEAM CLEANING METHOD: Again, this is not really steam cleaning. It uses hot water mixed with detergent then injected into the carpeting and sucked out as fast as it goes in. This method will leave your carpet a little more damp but it should do a good job on stained areas. Steam cleaning by professionals comes in two categories:

1. The PORTABLE CLEANING UNIT which is similar to what you can rent at the store, except the commercial is more powerful and will do a better job than what you can rent. The commercial portable carpet

cleaning system can handle nearly any type of dirt problem or soiled carpeting problem with a competent operator running it. Your carpet should look nearly new when finished.

2. The new TRUCK-MOUNTED STEAM CLEANING OUTFITS have been out for years, but like all new things have had to be tried and tested. The earlier machines broke down constantly and did not do the job they were designed to do. They also cost a great deal of money and there were a lot of frustrated cleaners who bought them, thinking they were going to get great results.

Today however, the industry—being an advancing and growing industry—have truck-mounted units that are very, very powerful, efficient and expensive.

As they are so expensive, you won't find these machines in every city or every part of the country. We recommend the newer models of truck-mounted steam cleaners (regardless of manufacturer) as the best way to get your carpets cleaned, as long as the operator knows what he is doing. An untrained operator could totally wreck your carpets—it would not be the machine's fault.

This goes back to selecting your carpet cleaner. Your carpeting is a big investment and you don't want to take too many chances with having the wrong people in your home goofing it up. We know of too many instances where the wrong people have done immeasurable harm to carpets. **We've** seen carpets shrunk as much as 3 inches off the wall, never again to be restretched. Carpet seams have fallen apart because people have been uninformed about the machines they are operating. Carpets are over soaked—a wet carpet is one thing, an over soaked carpet is another when the water squishes when you walk. This should never be allowed.

If friends don't have any good recommendations for you, go the Yellow Pages. Get the names of 2 or 3 that are close to you geographically. Ask for references. Look for truck-mounted high power cleaning machines first. If they are not available in your area, seek out portable steam cleaners. If you don't get satisfactory recommendations from the references, go to the other forms of carpet cleaning. They cannot hurt your carpet by inexperience or carelessness nearly as much as the truck-mounted equipment can by inexperienced or careless operators.

There is no way to pre-determine if a man knows his job because he doesn't have to tell you the truth. PAST WORK IS A MAN'S BEST RECOMMENDATION.

CARPET CLEANING
ADVERTISEMENTS

Carpet cleaners ads can be just as misleading as any other ads. Here then is some help.

1. ADS WITH COUPONS FOR SAVING DOLLARS ON YOUR CLEANING: These ads are good in a general sense but make sure you read the fine print. Usually the savings are good only for a specific amount of square feet or a specific group of rooms such as living room, dining room and hall. Also, there is a date by which you must redeem your coupon. Watch your paper regularly for ads of this kind to see if they aren't offering a coupon every week. If they are. It's just being used as a gimmick and shouldn't be taken seriously.

2. ADS WITH VALUABLE GUARANTEES:

If they offer a guarantee that states they will do only the best work that they know how to do with their type of equipment, it will be the most truthful guarantee. There is no way in the world that anybody can make a guarantee, of any value, without first seeing your carpet. Read guarantees very carefully. In past years in Southern California one large company ran ads with a guarantee that goes like this:

"Our expert crews will clean your carpet better than you have ever seen before or your money will be returned in full."

This claim on first reading says that their experts will come in and make your carpet look as good as new and they are so sure of it that they are willing to give back to you 100% of your money if they can't do it. "Wow, let's get to the phone!"

The guarantee actually reads: **"Our** guys will come out and clean your carpets, and because they have never been there before, it will be better than you've ever seen *them* clean your carpets."

So, because you did call them and you made an appointment (a matter of record which they can prove) and you invited them into your house and they performed a work designated by you, then you are under obligation to pay them. If you don't their company can sue you. You must pay (not really but they'll make you believe that you do) and after you've paid and the carpet has dried out enough for you to make a closer inspection, you find that you have been ripped off. Is it too late now? Not really, although you may never get your money back, you can still report them to the Better Business Bureau, and the local Chamber of Commerce, and write a letter to the local newspaper where you read the ad in the first place. If enough people write to their newspapers about these questionable business practices, they will refuse to run their ads for them.

3. THE SUPER CHEAP PRICE: In carpet cleaning ads you will always run across the super cheap price, something like "$24.95 for any 5 rooms in the house."

"Ridiculous," you say. Not really. People fall for this one all the time. Along with this ad the small print reads, "each additional room 10C per square foot." Just two small rooms at 10C per sq. ft. would amount to more than $24.95.

If you own a 4-bedroom house with a living room, dining room, and hall (hall is often considered a room), your bill is about $50. They will often charge you for heavy traffic area pre-spotting, "just another $10, Mam." Then, "How about the pre-conditioning that you'll need because your carpet is much more abused and soiled than what they normally run into? That's only $14.95 extra. And when they're done they'd be only to happy to give you this week's special on a soil retardant. Their regular price is 8° per sq. ft. but for this week only, it's just 5° per sq. ft. You only need it in the traffic areas—total price $18.50. It's really a bargain. Here's your bill, Mam, $93.40."

And you thought they were going to only charge you $24.95!

They also have hidden charges. Their ad states that the price includes moving furniture. They move it all right. Then you have to pay extra to have them move it back.

When you read an ad with a ridiculously low price for something, you can count on it not being exactly accurate. Just don't fall for it! The carpet cleaning industry has some real bandits in it. They'll take you for everything they can; and, on top of it, do a terrible job on your carpet.

HOW DO I FIND A PROFESSIONAL?

A professional will have good, modern carpet cleaning equipment and creditable name. If he's new to you, don't be afraid to ask for references in your own area. Then call those people. Try to *get at least* 2 out of 3 references. If 2 out of 3 were satisfied, he's probably OK. I say 2 out of 3 because some people expect their carpet to look like new after the carpet cleaner leaves and when it doesn't, they are not happy, and it's not necessarily the cleaner's fault.

If he should belong to a local or national Carpet Cleaning Organization, that is a plus for him, and also a guarantee for you. Generally, if a customer has a specific complaint, they can go to that organization if the businessman cannot satisfy their complaint. If the complaint is determined valid, that organization will do what it can to see that the customer is satisfied.

WHEN TO TAKE ADVANTAGE
OF A CLEANING SPECIAL

The two best times of the year for carpet cleaning specials are just before April 1 and November 1. The carpet cleaning business slows down during the winter months, so to get things going, the special will come out around April 1. They will surface again around November 1 because they want to make enough money to get them through the slow time.

If you should need your carpets cleaned, look for the specials at these times. Don't expect much in the summer. Summer time is the busiest time ever and a good carpet cleaner has his hands too full and overloaded to be offering any special deals to get more business.

WHAT ABOUT DYING
YOUR CARPETS

The dying of wall-to-wall carpeting has been tried and retried up until recently without any great success.

The problems that have to be overcome are threefold:

1. Trying to put a new color over an older color evenly and uniformly;

2. Putting coloring into a carpet that doesn't fade or wash out in the first or second cleaning; and

3. Being able to do the whole operation at a price that is less than replacing the carpet with all new carpet.

Within the last couple of years a new technique has been tried - resulting in a very successful dying, being costly yet effective.

The dying of your carpet should not be attempted unless you have proof that the dye will hold and that it will be uniform. The price is something that only you can determine if it's worth paying.

There is a sure method though of carpet dying but it is limited only to certain areas of the country. This is by going through your carpet retailer to the carpet mill dye house. You will be without a carpet for up to 2 or 3 weeks but if their dye house has the time and you have the money, you can be sure that it will come back to you done properly.

Bear in mind that if your carpet is old and the backing is becoming separated, the dye house will not take any responsibility for any part of the carpet except the color itself.

REPAIRING & MAKING
YOUR OWN SEAMS

Sometime in your life you will come across an opportunity to fix a seam in your carpeting. These seams are the places where your carpeting was literally glued (in some cases sewed) together. They are found in doorways and in any room that is wider and longer than 12 feet.

Most of the time these seams will never come undone but when they do there are reasons for it happening. When the carpet was installed, the installer may have had his seaming iron too hot or not hot enough. He may have moved his iron too fast or not fast enough.

This may have happened only on one small short part of the seam and unless a real strain was put on the seam it would never be discovered. Some strains that cause a seam to split are:

1. Cleaning where the carpet gets wet enough to shrink;

2. Dragging heavy furniture across a seam;

3. And, heavy traffic over a seamed area.

It is usually in doorways where a seam will first show signs of splitting.

If your carpeting has been down for more than one year, your carpet dealer who installed it is under no obligation to fix it. If he does, the charge will probably be minimal. But most people are living on carpet that they didn't purchase; therefore, the repair charge for a seam will be anywhere from $15 to $50, maybe even more if it is a serious split.

With the majority of these seam repairs, you can do it yourself and save the money. Here's how:

1. Clean the area under and around the loosened seam of all dirt, using the hose attachment of your vacuum cleaner.

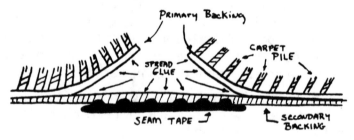

2. Seams that split usually do not open up so that you can see the pad underneath. The primary backing (refer to section on construction of carpet) has separated from the secondary backing.

3. After the area is cleaned, take CONTACT CEMENT (purchased at any hardware store) and a brush (usually comes in the small applicator bottle) and coat all inside surfaces.

Allow to dry 10 to 15 minutes before pressing the primary backing down into the secondary backing. You will have to hold these pieces up and away from each other during this drying time. When you do press them together, stand on it for a few minutes.

If there are any pieces of burlap sticking out from the seam, cut them off with scissors.

4. That's all there is to it. Again, a simple operation you can do yourself and save money.

MAKING YOUR OWN SEAMS

Items needed: A pair of scissors, burlap, and contact cement. (Most yardage stores have burlap. A yard will last a lifetime.)

1. Measure the length of the seam and cut a strip of burlap 3" wide and the length of your seam plus 4".

EXAMPLE: Let's say you have a seam to be made that is 13" long. Cut a piece of burlap 17" long and 3" wide.

The 4 extra inches are to extend 2 inches beyond the open seam on each end.

2. Take the Contact Cement and cover the 17" x 3" burlap piece. Allow to dry only 5 minutes before placing under the open seam. Once this burlap is in place, coat the back side of the carpet with Contact Cement and allow to dry 10 to 15 minutes. Press the carpet down onto the burlap and stand on it for a couple of minutes.

NOTE: You may use other glues, but first make certain that they will glue fabric and also that they are not water soluble.

3. For making your own seams, many carpet stores sell carpet tape that already has the glue on it. You simple press the carpet down onto it. It works but in NO WAY will it give you as good a bond as Contact Cement.

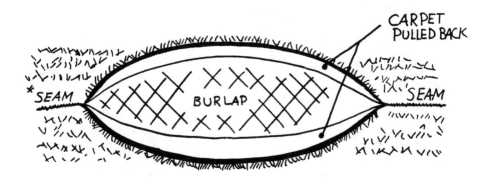

CAUTION All instructions for spot cleaning are for nylon and polyester carpets ONLY.

SPOTS & STAINS

Spots and stains should be cleaned immediately. Refer to stain chart for instruction on cleaning a variety of common household carpet stains.

One thing that seems to always happen to carpets is something will invariably be knocked over and spilled on the carpet. It might be a bowl of soup, gravy, cereal, whatever. Or an animal or child might become sick and throw up. These heavy spills need a speedy cleanup. That's the whole secret—the speed with which you get to that spill. Take care of these things as they happen. Don't just shove it aside and figure you can do it later. The longer most of these things lay on the carpet, the longer and harder it is to get out. THE TIME TO ACT IS NOW.

For instance, if stew is spilled, pick up all the solids first—all you can with a spoon. Work all the stew or gravy towards the center. Use a spoon and a butter knife or spatula to spread it into the spoon to get it up. After you have gotten up as much as possible, squeegee the carpet with the spoon to try to get it up. Then use a light detergent. (See Section on Vomit, page 79)

THE TOOL KIT: WHAT YOU NEED TO REPAIR AND GET OUT STAINS

Listed below are items that you should have set aside at home especially for most of your repair and spotting needs:

Razor Utility Knife

Scissors

Contact Cement (bottle)

Baking Soda

Sponge

1-Gallon Bucket

Old Tablespoon

Rubber Gloves

Vinegar (White)

Peroxide

Ammonia (Non-Detergent)

Liquid Detergent (Low Suds)

Rags

Paper Towels (all blotting is done with paper towels)

Brush (Reasonably Stiff)

1 Spray Bottle

1 Pint Perchlorethlene (Dry Clean Fluid purchased from local dry cleaner and put in a plastic squirt bottle)

1 Pint Lacquer Thinner

1 Pint Acetone

1 Medicine Dropper

Mix the cleaning fluid 1/3, the lacquer thinner 1/3, and the acetone 1/3. This solution is your main spot lifting tool after you have absorbed as much of the spilled mass as possible with rags. CAUTION:

This solution is highly flammable and should be kept in a safe place also out of the reach of young hands.

This mix is your general spotter and cleaning agent to be used in spray bottle or with medicine dropper.

CAUTION Before you clean any portion of your carpet, check first for color-fastness. This is done by saturating a white rag with ammonia and rubbing an area of carpet. If the color of the carpet comes off on the rag, don't use any strong cleaner on it.

HARD ONES FIRST

WAX: From time to time, wax will be found in the carpet for one reason or another. Getting it out is much more involved than putting it in but the process is the same. It had to melt first to get into the carpet; therefore, it must melt to come out, right?

Here's how to do it: Get a brown paper bag, the type you get your groceries in. If there is a lot of wax, you will need two large shopping bags. Next you will need an electric iron, the same as you use on your clothes except you will not need the steam mechanism so turn it of.

STEP 1.   Plug in iron and make sure not to set it on the carpet.

STEP 2.   Tear the bag open and make it flat. STEP 3. Place the paper over the wax.

STEP 4. Place the iron on top of the paper over the wax.

STEP 5.   Move the iron back and forth until you see the bag getting wet (turns dark) from the melting wax.

STEP 6.   Now move the paper over so that when you repeat Step 5, an all-together clean area of the paper will turn dark as the max melts.

STEP 7.   Repeat as many times as necessary until all the wax is out of the carpet and saturated into the paper.

CAUTION: Be certain not to allow the carpet to get overheated by using the iron for more than a couple of minutes at a time. Again, DO NOT PLACE THE IRON DIRECTLY ON THE CARPET.

GUM

If you get to it before it gets ground in, just use a pair of scissors to snip it off the fibers it is stuck to.

If it is ground in you will have some work ahead of you:

One way is to get an ice cube and hold it on the gum until the gum starts getting hard and brittle.

As this happens, you can use a sharp knife and chip it off.

Or, you can go to an electronics store and buy a spray can which contains a chemical that will freeze anything you spray with it. Then, chip it off with a sharp knife.

Or, use waterless handcleaner and massage it into the gum. As the gum becomes gooey, wipe it up with a soft rag. Be sure to use enough handcleaner to keep the gum gooey and slimy. After you're done, rinse the area several times with fresh water and use a towel or old diaper to absorb the moisture and the remaining handcleaner.

CIGARETTE BURNS & SPARKS
FROM THE FIREPLACE
(That have burned the carpet)

These small burns are really quite easy to fix. You will need a utility razor knife, scissors, and contact cement.

STEP 1.   Use the razor knife to scrape out the burned fabric—scrape it down to the top face of the primary backing.

STEP 2.   Take the contact cement and brush it onto the primary backing—be careful not to get it on the carpet pile.

STEP 3.   With the scissors, go into the closet and get a couple of pinches of carpet pile and carefully cut at the very base of the pile. Try to get pieces of tufted pile that will be approximately the same length as the rest of the yarns. Cut only what you think you will need to fill that particular burn hole.

STEP 4.   Holding these cut yarns in your hand, carefully but amply apply contactce ment to the yarn ends but don't apply the glue to both ends.

STEP 5.   Hold it in your hand for about 5 minutes—you might even blow on it. Then place it down into the burned spot, being careful not to let the glue touch the other carpet. Press it down with your hand and stand on it for about 5 minutes. DON'T MOVE YOUR FOOT AROUND.

STEP 6.   Wait now about 1/2 hour. Then fluff up the area with your hand. With the scissors, trim off any area that looks shabby.

URINE: CAT & DOG

This is the hardest area to cover because most people don't want to hear the truth. If an animal urinates in your house more than a couple of times to the point that it is a habit, or to the point that you can smell it, you may as well figure on throwing out the whole thing—CARPET, PAD, ANIMALS. The real facts are that if a dog has urinated more than a few times, you have only a 50% chance of getting rid of the odor. If a cat does it more than a few times, you only have a 10% chance. No, I don't hate cats. We have three of them. Those are just the facts. Both animals can totally destroy carpeting in just a couple of weeks if allowed to.

I won't deal with the dog and cat problem because the answer to those problems are simple—replace it all. I'll stick to the occasional accident.

Pet stores have a variety of sprays that sometimes work. After you have discovered the puddle, blot it up with a towel and then rinse thoroughly with water several times, using a mild ammonia mixture with the rinse water. Then spray this stuff on it. Or you might sprinkle on baking powder, let dry and vacuum it up. Then put some powdered carpet deodorant on the carpet. Some people will put vinegar in the carpet, but that leaves a vinegar odor. You might also try a product called "C.D.^{2TM}" It's expensive but it works the best of all. You can find this in some of the larger chain drug stores. This is about the best procedure you might expect to do. With urine, there just isn't a surefire method.

RUST

When rust is discovered you have several options for removal. If the stain is just on the surface you may cut it off with scissors. If the stain is really down into the pile you could either treat it like a cigarette burn (as described in CIGARETTE BURN SECTION). Or you may purchase an acid solution from a janitorial supply or in some large super markets or variety stores. There are different named products, so just ask someone and tell them what you're looking for. **CAUTION:** Be sure to follow instructions that are printed on the container. It is very dangerous acid and can be quite harmful. It might be noted also that the rust stain will usually re-appear after several months and will then have to be treated again. (Do not use on wool.)

BLOOD

Mix: 2 Tablespoons of powder detergent

1 Quart of Warm Water

1/2 Cup of Ammonia

Saturate a rag in this mixture and massage it in the area until you have the majority of blood up. Rinse the rag with fresh cool water and rinse the carpet area. Sprinkle on medicinal peroxide. Wait until the bubbling stops, then rinse with fresh clean water as above. Blot up with a paper towel. Repeat the whole process as needed.

WINE (RED OR WHITE)

Blot up with a paper towel as soon as possible. Rinse with cold water mixed with ammonia (1/2 cup to 1 qt. water). Blot again with paper towel and pour table salt on the spilled area. Lay a damp paper towel on top of the salt Leave it there for about 12 hours. Then vacuum up the salt.

COFFEE-TEA

Mix water (1 cup) and detergent (1 tablespoon low-sudsing) and pour on spot. Blot with paper towel. Sprinkle white vinegar on it and rinse with cool water. Blot with a paper towel. Sprinkle straight ammonia on and blot.

VOMIT

Wipe up the main mass. With rubber gloves on, saturate a rag with the cleaning solution (see Kit List) and massage it into spot until all the area has been covered. Wipe up and rinse with cool water, blot with towel. Mix low-suds detergent (1 Table-spoon) ammonia (2 Tablespoons) and hot water (1 cup). Rinse spot and blot. Rinse and blot again.

MODEL GLUE, HOUSEHOLD GLUE & NAIL POLISH

Use a nail polish remover with the eyedropper and use paper towels as with the lipstick. Repeat, then rinse and blot.

BALL-POINT INK — GRAVY — FURNITURE POLISH (NON-STAIN) CRAYONS — BUTTER — ASPHALT MASCARA — LATEX PAINT PASTE SHOEWAX — TAR

All of the above are handled the same way. Use rubber gloves and put in as much cleaning fluid mix as may be needed to get up whatever size spot you have. Then with a paper towel, wipe or blot out what you can. Repeat the process, then use a detergent (1 Tablespoon) and hot water mixture (1 cup)-blot-rinse-blot-rinse-blot. For ball point & crayon you can spray hair spray on it first then wipe with paper towel.

COUGH SYRUP

Same as above except in between the detergent/ ammonia action and the rinsing, add vinegar (sprinkle on the spot). Allow to sit 10 - 15 minutes before proceeding to the rinsing stage.

RED BERRIES — FRUIT JUICES & BAR DRINKS CATSUP — CHOCOLATE — ICE CREAM OR MILK PRODUCTS — TOOTHPASTE

Use 1 cup warm water, 1 Tablespoon ammonia and regular detergent, 2 tablespoons, mixture and work in with towel. Rinse and blot. Then repeat-rinse-blot-rinse-blot. If any stains from berries, chocolate or catsup are left, use the salt method for wine stains.

LIPSTICK

Take a small cup and put 1 Tablespoon of cleaning fluid in it. With rubber gloves on and some paper towels at hand, drop solution just on the lipstick only. Give it a chance to dissolve the lipstick. After it is done, use the paper towels to get the lipstick up. Do not spread around. Concentrate only on the yarns that have lipstick on them.

ANY QUESTIONS? PLEASE WRITE!

If there are any other stains not covered here and a professional is not able to help with the problem, please feel free to write us a letter. Include in the information: what caused the stain; if it was a brand name product; the type of carpet - fabric brand name; approximate age of the carpet.

We'll get a reply off to you as soon as we can.

Consumers Floor Covering Research Service Route 6 Box 67

Foyotteville, Tenn. 37334

THE DO-IT-YOURSELF
TILE FLOOR

I almost hesitate to include this section because of the total disasters that people have managed to do themselves while attempting to become floor tile experts.

It's been my contention that if you don't know how to do something, get somebody to do it for you who does know or at least have him teach you in person.

Today, however, more and more people are putting down their own tile floors. Also more and more tile companies are making floor tiles with the self-stick (by the way they really do stick) so that people can do it themselves.

Well, it's hard to teach somebody a trade like tile laying in a book. But because 1 out of every 20 of you will eventually try if for yourself, I'll try to give you enough information and directions to make your job the best on the block for the least amount of money.

Let's start with the product. The name brand is VERY IMPORTANT here. Pay a little extra but get a good national brand name. Some bargain discount stores offer their own brands or some off-the-wall, who-ever-heard-of-it brand. Many major companies make floor tile and will stand behind their products (G.A.F.™, Armstrong™, Kentile™, Azroc™, etc.).

Before you buy, you'll have to determine HOW MUCH TO BUY. Tiles will usually come in 1' x 1' squares in a box of 45. You can cover 45 square feet of floor space with one box. Because of waste on edge cuts, you should allow at least a 6% waste factor. Let's say you are going to tile your kitchen which is 125 square feet. You will need 125 square feet divided by 45 per box or 2 boxes and 35 tiles, but you must allow that 6% so 125 X .06 = 8 tiles or a total of 133 total tiles. To be on the safe side, buy 2 more tiles and make it exactly 3 boxes.

Now, bring it all home and sit the 3 boxes separately on the floor close to the kitchen. Don't put them outside or in the garage unless you don't plan on doing this job for awhile. Be certain to have those tiles in the house at least 24 hours before you start to install. It is also important to have the temperature no lower than 65 degrees and keep it there or higher for 3 to 5 days after the tile job is done.

These directions are only FOR SELF-STICK TILE. They' are very good tiles and when you're done, nobody will know the difference.

You will need only a couple of tools unless you run into some problems. You must have a steel tape measure, a chalk line, red, white or blue chalk, a pencil, a rolling pin, a sharp razor utility knife, and a steel straight edge. Those are the tools you'll need for only the installation. Other tools will be called for as we go along.

PREPARATIONS FOR THE CONCRETE SLAB FLOOR

If the floor you are covering is on a slab floor, most of the trouble has already been eliminated.

STEPS: 1. Remove any furniture or any object from floor (refrigerator, chairs, table, etc.)

2. Remove all wood molding from the cabinets that border along the floor and also any wall molding that is touching the floor.

3. If there is carpeting that will touch any part of your proposed floor, you will have to pry up the metal strip that is holding the

carpet down. Once this strip is lifted, it will be of no further value and will need to be replaced. Be certain that when you purchase the new metal strip to get enough concrete nails 1/2 inch long to put it back down again over the new tile.

4. Now, it's time to lift up that old floor you want to replace. You will need a flat scraping hoe or long handle ice scraper or some similar tool. If it is tile you are lifting, it will break off and chip as you go. It's a tough job but be patient and get it all. If it's sheet vinyl that's coming up, it will tend to tear or rip; but again, be patient to get it all up. This really is the toughest part of the job as far as strenuous labor. After this you shouldn't sweat again until you try to put those concrete nails down to anchor your carpet metal. But that will be the last job and after that you'll be done. Except of course, to put your refrigerator back in without scratching up your new floor. Get help for that one and use a dolly.

Now, back to floor preparation. A CLEAN FLOOR is the number one secret in a good and proper tile installation so take all precautions to strip that concrete bare of everything. Use a wire brush to get up any hard-to-get parts.

After all things are removed and the floor has been swept and damp mopped, you should now check for any holes, cracks, or chips that may be in the concrete. If there are any, mix up a small batch of plaster mix and fill the holes, etc., with a wide blade putty knife. Allow to dry completely, then scrape smooth and use a medium grade sand paper to make each patched area perfectly flush with the rest of the floor.

Sweep again and wash now with a warm water and tri-sodium phosphate cleaner. Then rinse thoroughly and allow to dry COMPLETELY. It is also EXTREMELY IMPORTANT to have NO PARTICLES of ANYTHING on the floor. Now you are ready to install.

PREPARATIONS FOR THE WOOD FLOOR

Now, of course, if nothing goes wrong, the preparations for the wooden floor will be exactly the same as for concrete unless the floor is lose or moves when you walk on it. It would not be wise to put down tile on a floor that moves because it will probably work itself loose with all the motion. You won't have to use a cleaner on wood, but you will probably have a lot of repair work to perform on the wood to make it smooth. A good belt sander may be necessary to accomplish this. In those areas hard to get, use a sanding block with a rough sandpaper. After the wood floor has been swept and dry-mopped, it must be allowed to dry. This may take some time but be sure that it is totally dry before you place down your tiles. Also if you should live in a mobile home and you have a particle board floor, it would be advisable to cover the entire floor with 1/4 inch **ACX** plywood underlay-ment. With a particle board floor in an area that may have water spilled on it, the tiles will come up and the floor will dissolve.

If the floor is loose you should take extra measures to nail it down and it may be necessary to add extra support braces underneath. If the floor squeaks when you walk on it, locate the squeak and use "Lub-A-Lite™". Most Lumber and large hardware stores carry it or something similar.

Now you're ready to install the tiles.

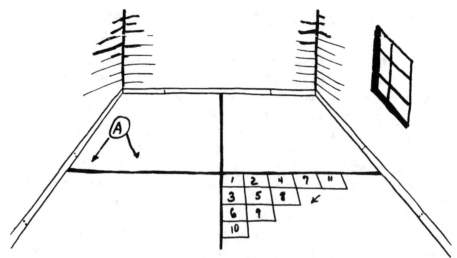

1. FIND THE EXACT CENTER OF EACH WALL, IN THE ROOM YOU ARE TILING. WITH THE HELP OF A FRIEND-SNAP YOUR CHALK LINE FROM CENTER TO CENTER (A) AND WHERE THE 2 LINES MEET WILL BE THE FLOOR CENTER.

2. START FROM THE CENTER POINT, LAYING DOWN TILES IN ONE QUARTER OF THE ROOM—FOLLOW THE NUMBERS OF INSTALLATION ABOVE—BE VERY CERTAIN TO KEEP THE TILES LINED UP ON THE CHALK LINE. TILES WITH ARROWS PRINTED ON THE BACK OF EACH TILE SHOULD ALWAYS BE SET GOING THE SAME DIRECTION. AS YOU PUT DOWN THE TILES MAKE SURE NOT TO MOVE YOUR KNEES AROUND SO AS THE TILES WILL BE MOVED FROM THEIR ORIGINAL POSITION.

3. FINISH THE ENTIRE QUARTER SECTION BUT DON'T DO THE FINAL TILE THAT WILL GO AROUND THE EDGE UNTIL ALL OTHER QUARTERS HAVE BEEN COMPLETED.

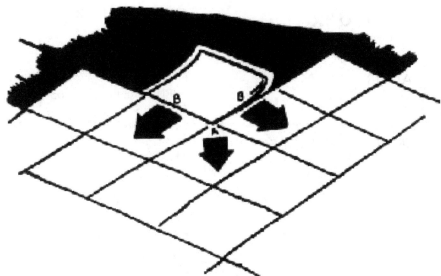

AS YOU PLACE THE TILE INTO POSITION PUT CORNER (A) INTO A TIGHT FIT. ONCE THE TILE IS FLAT USE BOTH HANDS PRESSED DOWN ON THE TILE AND PUSHING TOWARDS THE (B) ARROWS. BE PATIENT AND IT WILL COME OUT LOOKING GREAT. PLEASE DON'T GET IN A HURRY REMEMBER: "THE HURRIER I GO THE BEHINDER I GET."

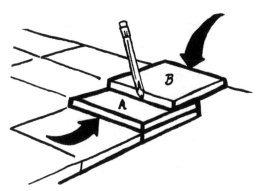

NOW START ON THE EDGES. WORK IN ONE DIRECTION ONLY AS YOU GET TO DOOR WAYS AND CORNERS CUT EACH TILE TO FIT ITS OWN PARTICULAR POSITION. TO CUT YOUR EDGE TILES— PLACE A WHOLE TILE (do not take the paper off the bottom) OVER THE LAST TILE NEXT TO THE WALL (A) THEN TAKE ANOTHER TILE (don't remove paper) AND SET IT UP AGAINST THE WALL (B). TAKE A PENCIL & SCRIBE YOUR CUT LINE ON (A). NOW CUT TILE A WITH RAZOR KNIFE & STRAIGHT EDGE. PUT (A) IN PLACE. GREAT!

TAKE YOUR ROLLING PIN AND ROLL OVER THE ENTIRE FLOOR WITH LOTS OF PRESSURE. THIS WILL MAKE THE TILES EVEN AND, MORE IMPORTANT, MAKE SURE THAT THE TILES ARE STUCK TO THE GLUE FIRMLY.

Index

Printed in the USA
CPSIA information can be obtained
at www.ICGtesting.com
LVHW012005020624
782068LV00001B/85

9 780894 960581